HAWAIIAN JOURNEY

IMAGES OF YESTERYEAR

An Illustrated Narrative of the History of the Islands

by Joseph G. Mullins

Mutual Publishing

Economic change came more slowly to O'ahu's outlying districts, districts such as Wai'anae. Yet, even this traditional rural area was being transformed when the Wai'anae Sugar Plantation Company under Herman Widermann opened in 1878. By the mid-1880s Wai'anae was the largest settlement on O'ahu outside of Honolulu, and included not only the plantation, but a mill, a manager's house (seen in the photo), several stores owned by Native Hawaiians and Chinese, two churches, two schools, a clubhouse, and, later, a train station. [Hawai'i State Archives]

Mutual Publishing, LLC
1215 Center Street, Suite 210
Honolulu, Hawai'i 96816
Ph: (808) 732-1709
Fax: (808) 734-4094
Email: info@mutualpublishing.com
www.mutualpublishing.com

Mutual Publishing

Visitors to Honolulu toward the end of the nineteenth century frequently remarked on the cosmopolitan and American character of the bustling port. While the grog shops, saloons, brothels, gambling halls, and opium dens still flourished, Honolulu also boasted an opera house, first-class hotels, the Royal Hawaiian Theater, a Waikīkī tourist retreat with bathhouses and amusements, and a racetrack and gardens at Kapi'olani Park. Electric lights, telephones, trolleys, and clean, clear pumped water for households enriched the lives of residents. At the time of this view of Honolulu Harbor, circa 1892, sailing ships still prevailed but steam was rapidly taking over. [Hawai'i State Archives]

Ali'iolani Hale (House of the Heavenly Chief) was originally designed as a palace for Kamehameha V, but the plans were altered to create an administration building across from the palace. Built of concrete blocks, at that time a fairly new material, it was completed in 1874. It contained the kingdom's House of Nobles, House of Representatives, the Supreme Court and Judiciary Department, the Law Library, and the National Museum of the Hawaiian Kingdom. To the left is Kapuāiwa, the Board of Health building, completed in 1884. On the far right is a portion of the opera house, completed in 1881 at the corner of Mililani and King streets. [Hawai'i State Archives]

Table of Contents

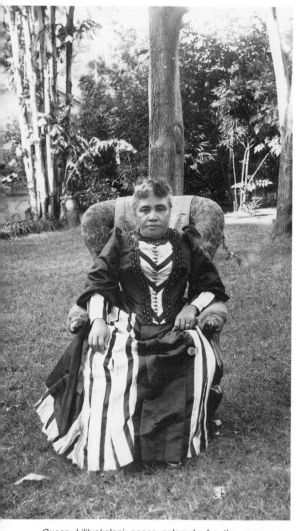

Queen Lili'uokalani poses solemnly for the camera on the grounds of Washington Place in 1893, following the overthrow of the monarchy. Standing nearby is her faithful supporter Samuel Nowlein, who in January 1895 would join Robert Wilcox in an aborted attempt to restore the queen to the throne. [Baker–Van Dyke Collection]

After the annexation of Hawai'i in 1898, Queen Lili'uokalani rarely made public appearances. On December 15, 1911, she agreed to attend the dedication of Pearl Harbor, where she sat in quiet dignity amidst the American military and civilian authorities. During World War I, the queen ordered the American flag to be raised over Washington Place for the first time when she learned that several Hawaiian soldiers had been killed in action. [Hawai'i State Archives]

Traversing the Pali. [Hawai'i State Archives]

In 1849, Dr. Jerrett Judd, a physician missionary who became secretary of state to Kamehameha III, traveled abroad to negotiate treaties. He was accompanied by the young Liholiho (left), and the young Lot (right). [Hawai'i State Archives]

After settling at Kalaupapa, Father Damien posed with the members of the St. Philomena Choir. Believing that Hansen's disease was brought to the Islands by Chinese immigrants, Hawaiians called the terrible affliction Ma'i Pākē, the Chinese sickness. Circa 1875. [Hawai'i State Archives]

Preface

Hawaiian Journey originally appeared under the title *Hawaii 1776–1976* to commemorate Hawai'i's participation in the nation's bicentennial observance. It enjoyed instant popularity among both local residents and visitors to the Islands. Now, to reach a wider audience, this completely revised and updated softcover edition has been prepared.

Readers who take delight in vintage photographs will find many additional nostalgic pictures, some of which have had only limited circulation.

There has also been some reorganiz- ation: the sections entitled Statehood and Islands in Transition have been combined and rewritten, and the Downtown section has been re-titled Old Honolulu to permit broader coverage. Throughout the book additional narrative has been provided.

In the selection of topics, historical importance was not the sole consideration. The more subjective factor of what makes for interesting storytelling was given equal weight. The availability of photographs also influenced the selection. However, all the major events and personalities that belong in an overview of Hawaiian history have been included.

The narrative is based on the facts that are available, although not everyone may agree with the interpretation. In researching the material, it was found that even the experts disagree. Since this is not meant to be a definitive or original work of Hawaiian history, it will not settle any controversy, although the material presented here has been carefully researched.

Hawaiian Journey is intended to serve as a nostalgic introduction to Hawai'i's unique story. Hopefully it will contribute to that special pride felt by all who live in these Islands.

This memorable photograph was taken at a lū'au held at the Henry Poor residence in Waikīkī in February 1889. At center is King David Kalākaua. On his right are Princess Lili'uokalani (later Queen) and writer Robert Louis Stevenson. Seated at the king's left is Mrs. Thomas Stevenson, mother of the famed writer. The lū'au was an important feature of Hawaiian culture; it symbolized welcome and hospitality for the visitor. With everyone seated on the floor or the ground, it was certainly an easy way to put all at ease in getting to know each other. Despite the presence of kings, princesses, and renowned luminaries, a lū'au is, by its very nature, a relaxed setting where enjoyment of food and good conversation takes precedence over formality.
[Baker–Van Dyke Collection]

Hawai'i's history in story and legend is ancient and proud, dating back at least a thousand years before the American colonies became a nation in 1776. It is likely that neither the exact date when Polynesian people first set foot on these Islands, nor much detail about events occurring between that date and the first contact with Europeans, will ever be known. The Hawaiians were a people who preserved their history orally, through chants and legends. Much of that early history disappeared as the Hawaiian population, and use of the Hawaiian language, declined during the nineteenth and twentieth centuries.

Modern Hawaiian history begins on January 20, 1778, when Captain James Cook's expedition made its first contact with the Hawaiian people on the islands of Kaua'i and Ni'ihau. On that day, Hawai'i's long isolation from the world beyond its horizons came to an end, beginning a most colorful, and sometimes tragic, chapter of our nation's history. Certainly it was the most unusual. Beginning with a traditional Polynesian society, Hawai'i evolved through an almost bewildering series of cultural and social events that included nationhood; contact with Western technology and ideas; population decline; massive in-migration of non-Polynesians; overthrow of the monarchy; a short-lived republic; annexation as a U.S. territory; World War II; and statehood.

Although Captain Cook was English, Hawai'i's proximity to the U.S. resulted in an early American interest and influence that eventually culminated in statehood. While there were sporadic attempts by the British and the French to bring the Islands into their spheres of influence, the American presence was always dominant. American whaling fleets began wintering in Hawai'i as early as 1819, and by 1844 as many as 490 American whaling ships crowded Honolulu and Lahaina waters. Protestant missionaries from Puritan New England arrived in 1820 to leave a peculiarly American imprint on Hawai'i's society and attitudes. At any one time during the Hawaiian monarchy, the majority of foreigners residing in the Islands were Americans.

Major events in American history invariably affected Hawai'i. The California Gold Rush of 1849 stimulated Hawaiian agriculture, and high prices were paid for Hawaiian sugar, vegetables, and meat. Several years later the American Civil War sparked a dramatic expansion of Hawai'i's sugar industry to supply the North when it was cut off from Southern sugar. The Spanish-American War, from which the U.S. gained bases in the Philippines and Guam, crystallized American military opinion about Hawai'i's strategic central Pacific location. Annexation of Hawai'i to the U.S. followed rapidly. The Japanese attack on Pearl Harbor proved a tragic confirmation of Hawai'i's strategic value. Today, Hawai'i continues to be the nation's bastion of defense in the Pacific.

Because of this early and lasting American influence, Hawai'i's social and economic institutions became patterned after those of the U.S., a process accelerated by the fact that significant American contact began at a time when the Hawaiian culture was rapidly disintegrating. Yet there were always differences.

Hawai'i's record of assimilating people of different ethnicities and nationalities was unequaled by any other state in the Union. Today, almost fifty percent of Hawai'i's marriages are between people of different ethnicities. Hawai'i's culture still retains aspects of its Polynesian heritage along with an unmistakable Asian influence. The fact that Hawai'i is an island group also had an effect. Local lifestyles and values are shaped by the Islands' three thousand-nautical-mile isolation from the American continent as well as by the varied ethnic backgrounds and intermingling of its ethnic groups. As a result, Hawai'i's people have always felt different from their continental cousins.

This sense of uniqueness is now being endangered by rapid economic development, urbanization, and increased population growth—all of which threaten to erode Hawai'i's romantic charm and natural beauty. The threat of cultural erosion has permeated Hawaiian history ever since contact with Westerners began. But, if the broad sweep of Hawaiian history suggests anything, it is that the Island ways of doing and perceiving things will survive conformist pressures and that Hawai'i will retain much of its cherished uniqueness and special way of life.

Hawaiian words have sometimes been pluralized to ease the sentence flow. Since the Hawaiian language is not foreign in Hawai'i, its words are not italicized.

All numbers and figures are from the State of Hawai'i's Department of Business, Economic Development & Tourism. The island of Hawai'i is referred to as the Big Island.

Polynesian explorers strike out boldly across unknown seas in search of new land. At least two thousand years of accumulated navigational expertise contributed to their confidence. Their ancestors usually found an island somewhere beyond the horizon, though many an expedition must have perished when land did not appear. To accomplish long voyages over an immense and lonely sea to thinly scattered islands, the Polynesians developed a technological marvel—the seagoing double canoe, which often reached between eighty and one hundred feet in length. It can more aptly be described as a ship, consisting of two hulls with a platform lashed between to provide living, cooking, and work space, and room to transport food, plants, and domesticated animals. Lacking instruments of navigation or charts of any kind, the Polynesians sailed into vast oceans. Far from the secure landfalls of nearby continents, they staked their lives on their intimate knowledge of the sky and its stars, the sea and its currents, the flight of birds, and many other natural signs. In this Herb Kane painting, a canoe approaches the Big Island during a volcanic erruption. [© Herb Kawainui Kane]

Captain Cook was not the first man to "discover" the Hawaiian Islands; he was the first known European to arrive. Hawai'i was first settled by migrants from the Marquesas. The first settlement may have been as early as 300 to 800 AD; archaeologists differ as to dating. Some historians believe that there was a second migration, around 1100 AD, from the Society Islands, and a time of voyaging back and forth. According to this narrative, contact with southern Polynesia soon ceased as the newcomers adapted to their large and lightly settled islands. Other historians believe that the second migration is only myth, and that Hawaiian society developed entirely from the first period of Marquesan settlement.

To accomplish long voyages over an immense and lonely sea to thinly scattered islands, the Polynesians developed a technological marvel—the seagoing double canoe, which often reached between eighty and one hundred feet in length. It can more aptly be described as a ship, consisting of two hulls with a platform lashed between to provide living, cooking, and work space, and room to transport food, plants, and domesticated animals.

Lacking instruments of navigation or charts of any kind, the Polynesians sailed into vast oceans. Far from the secure landfalls of nearby continents, they staked their lives on their intimate knowledge of the sky and its stars, the sea and its currents, the flight of birds, and many other natural signs.

Plunged for centuries into isolation from the outside world, the Hawaiians developed a unique cultural heritage based on customs brought with them from the south and ways developed in their new land. This was the civilization that Captain Cook met when he came upon the Hawaiian Islands.

In the centuries before the arrival of Captain Cook, Hawaiian society was a highly stratified system with strictly maintained castes. As in other Polynesian nations, each caste had its assigned tasks and responsibilities. Not until 1810 was there a single king who ruled over all Hawai'i. Before then, there were a number of small kingdoms that divided the islands and were often at war with each other.

In each of these small kingdoms, ka moi, the king, headed the social pyramid, assisted by a chief minister and a high priest. Next in ranking were the ali'i, or chiefs, who varied in power depending on ancestral lineage and ability. Persons specially trained in the memorization of genealogies were important members of a chief's retinue because a chief's ranking in society was determined by the legitimacy of his genealogy. Chiefs ruled over portions of the land at the whim of the king, who could remove and replace them at will.

Below the chiefs but above the commoners were the kahuna, or experts. They were the priests, the sorcerers, the healers, and craftsmen. Kahunas such as priests and sorcerers were feared for their mysterious powers and arcane knowledge. Skilled healers and craftsmen were also highly regarded; they knew their trades as well as the rituals and prayers that ensured success in their endeavors.

The majority of Hawai'i's people were maka'āinana or commoners, subjects of the chief upon whose land they lived. They did most of the hard work: building fishpond walls and housing, fishing, farming, and making tapa cloth. The commoners paid taxes both to the king and to their chief and provided warriors for the chief's army. These taxes took the form of food, clothing, and other products. Unlike medieval serfs, commoners were not bound forever to the territory and ruler. If they wished, they could change allegiance to the chief of another land, but they first had to find a chief, or community, willing to accept them.

Below the commoners were a numerically small group of people known as kauwā or outcasts. Little is known of their origins or of their true role in Hawaiian society, although they were believed to be slaves of the lowest order.

The "glue" that cemented the ancient social structure was the kapu system. The word, known in English as "taboo," meant sacred or prohibited; the laws were taken so seriously that violators were swiftly punished by being strangled or clubbed to death. The daily world of old Hawai'i was filled with kapu. A commoner had to be careful lest his shadow fall across the person of a high chief, and he had to be quick to kneel or lie down in the presence of such sacred persons. Birth, death, faulty behavior, the building of a canoe, and many other activities were regulated by this system, which permeated all aspects of ancient Hawaiian life.

Heiau or Hawaiian temples contained images which symbolized the gods. Through prayer and the proper presentation of offerings, the people either sought the help of or placated the anger of the gods. There were a great number of minor gods associated with all of the occupations but they were mostly variations of the four major gods (who represented the universal forces) known as Kū, Kanaloa, Lono, and Kāne. Commoners performed their own simple ceremonies to family or personal gods called 'aumakua while the complicated religious life of the ali'i required the services of kahuna in large temple complexes. In some temples, human sacrifices took place.

Kānaka Maoli, People of Old

The woman is beating wauke, or mulberry bark, to make tapa, which was used for clothing and blankets. Tapa, known also as kapa, can best be described as a kind of soft, pliable paper. Tapa was decorated in various colors using natural plant and shellfish dyes, with geometric designs applied by block-printing. Hawaiians carried the art of tapa decoration to a high state, using more colors and designs than any other Polynesian people. Mats, blankets, and a huge old-style wooden surfboard lie about the compound. What appears to be a metal bucket may be a sign of encroaching Western influence. So might the wooden table and the doorways of the houses. However, the artists of the day sometimes took considerable liberties with the facts. [Hawai'i State Archives]

A View in O'whyee, with one of the Priest's Houses. This quaintly titled engraving shows a Hawaiian village scene still untouched by the influence of the outside world. The word "O'whyhee" is one of several attempts to spell "Hawaii" in English before the Hawaiian language was put in written form by a committee of early missionaries. There were no true cities or towns in old Hawai'i. People gathered in kauhale, or small coastal villages near good fishing grounds or beside fertile land where they grew taro and sweet potatoes, two staples of their diet. The homes of commoners had earthen floors covered with dry grasses and lauhala mats, while the homes of higher-ranking Hawaiians were often raised on a stone foundation platform, and the floor was covered with small, smooth pebbles. [Hawai'i State Archives]

Kānaka Maoli, People of Old

The canoes of fishermen and traveling visitors are drawn up on the beach beside a Hawaiian seaside village. The dim profile of the distant headland suggests Diamond Head, thus locating this village in the general area of Waikīkī. Most Hawaiian villages were located near the sea although there were some large inland villages, particularly in the uplands of the Big Island. Captain Cook described a Kaua'i village as follows: "Though they seem to have adopted the mode of living in villages, there is no appearance of defense, or fortification near any of them; and the houses are scattered about, without any order, either with respect to their distances from each other, or their position in any particular direction. Neither is there any proportion as to their size.... Their figure is not unlike oblong corn, or hay-stacks; and they are well thatched with long grass, which is laid on slender poles, disposed with some regularity. The entrance is made indifferently in the end or side, and is an oblong hole, so low, that one must rather creep than walk in; and is often shut up by a board or planks, fastened together, which serves as a door, but having no hinges, must be removed occasionally. They are kept remarkably clean; their floors are covered with a large quantity of dried grass, over which they spread mats to sleep upon...." [Hawai'i State Archives]

Capital punishment in ancient Hawai'i. Criminals and violators of kapu were punished by strangulation or clubbing. Sometimes abuses of power took place when an arrogant chief ordered the execution of a commoner who displeased him in some way. The fear of sudden and final punishment helped the kahuna and the ali'i to keep the common people obedient. [Hawai'i State Archives]

A young Hawaiian girl dressed in the traditional kihei cape made of tapa. This engraving was made in the early decades of the nineteenth century. [Hawai'i State Archives]

Interior of a Hawaiian chieftain's hut. This engraving was made shortly after Western contact with Hawai'i when outside influence was still minor. A retainer, carrying a small feather kahili or symbol of nobility, looks after the chief's comfort as household women relax nearby. [Hawai'i State Archives]

Kānaka Maoli, People of Old

John Webber, official artist on Cook's third voyage, was interested in recording every possible detail of the new lands and peoples they encountered. This is one of the most unusual recorded sights: a double-hulled sailing canoe manned by masked Hawaiians. The helmet-mask was made of a gourd; the masks may have been worn for religious reasons. [Hawai'i State Archives]

Tattooing was an important art form in most ancient Polynesian societies, and in some areas people were heavily tattooed over almost their entire body. Among the Maoris of New Zealand, facial tattooing was extremely complex while among Samoans the decorations were concentrated between the knees and the waist. Tahiti and the Marquesas were among the island groups where the art reached a high state of complexity. The English word tattoo is a direct borrowing from the Marquesan "tatu" or the Tahitian "tatau" by sailors who picked up the word and established it in our vocabulary. The practice of tattooing was less widespread in Hawai'i, yet the Hawaiians created numerous designs including birds, plant motifs, and geometric patterns such as the checkerboard style seen on this chieftain. The tattooed words on his arm read "TAMAAHMAH [Kamehameha], died May 8, 1819." Upon the King's death, people throughout the kingdom commemorated the event in the newly learned alphabet. The young man in this drawing wears a large cape made of thousands of tiny feathers tied in bundles of three to a cord mesh. Such cloaks were a status symbol worn only by high-ranking personages. Additional proof of rank is demonstrated by his feather-covered helmet. Hawaiian helmets resembled those worn by the classical Greeks and Romans. [Hawai'i State Archives]

Frances Williams Olmstead, Incidents of a Whaling Voyage 1841. [Baker-Van Dyke Collection]

Surfing fascinated foreign artists who, unfamiliar with this distinctive sport, were sometimes inaccurate in illustrating it. Early boards were five to fifteen feet long and were crafted into elongated "tombstone" shapes and stained with the pounded bark of kukui nut trees. [Baker–Van Dyke Collection]

Body surfing (without a surfboard) may have been known on many islands in Polynesia; a rudimentary form of surfing may even have been enjoyed in Tahiti and the other Society Islands. But surfing as a sport came into full flower in ancient Hawai'i.

Like other aspects of life in old Hawai'i, the act of surfing was imbued with spiritual significance. Just to create the surfboard, one had to select the proper tree, prepare the wood, and shape the board following the proper rituals. Even the launching of the board into the sea for the first time was done with appropriate ceremony. The hope was that, if one followed these rituals, the gods would grant success to the board and its owner.

There were two kinds of surfboards in use in old Hawai'i, a shorter board called the alaia and a longer one known as the olo. The shorter alaia was used in riding waves closer to shore, while the olo was ridden in the big waves further out. Generally, the smaller alaia boards were made of koa or breadfruit wood, which was heavy compared to the light wiliwili wood of the longer olo boards.

It was typical of the hierarchical society of old Hawai'i that the common people could not use the superior wiliwili wood for their surfboards and had to be content with the heavy and less buoyant koa. Thus, the ali'i had better boards, and they placed a kapu on the best surfing beaches. Also, because the ali'i were typically larger and stronger than the general population and had more leisure to develop their physique and their surfing skills, they often became the best surfers.

Old surfboards were bigger, heavier, and more difficult to handle than the boards of today. They did not have a skeg, the small, stern-side rudder. Some of the ancient boards in museum collections are eighteen feet or more in length and weigh more than 150 pounds.

After the arrival of the missionaries in 1820, surfing went into a steep decline and almost disappeared as a sport. The missionaries considered surfing to be a waste of time better spent in work or prayer. In 1874, when King Kalākaua ascended the throne of Hawai'i, surfing became popular again, only to disappear once more after his death. But in the early 1900s Hawai'i's economy improved, and there was an increase of interest in sports. Canoe and surfing clubs were formed and enthusiasm spread among young people of all backgrounds. Soon the waters off Waikīkī were crowded with Hawai'i's youth enjoying surfing and improving their skills on the waves.

Hula

Many of the original sketches made by early European artists who came to Hawai'i with various expeditions were later retouched by copyists who changed the body and facial appearance of the Hawaiians to conform to the continental idea of beauty. But in this engraving by Choris, the Hawaiian male dancers seem to be accurately depicted. The dancers carry elaborately decorated feather-embellished gourd rattles, and wear dog-tooth anklets which make distinctive rattling sounds as they perform. Bracelets of large boar tusks decorate their wrists, contributing to the visual impact of the arm movements. The man in the center is heavily tattooed from forehead to waist. Such tattooing was widespread in ancient Polynesia, and the Hawaiians developed very specialized designs. The dancers do not wear customary malo (men's loin cloths) but seem to be wearing intricately wrapped tapa cloth or even imported cotton cloth from a trading ship. In the background, the musicians accompany the dancers, beating gourd drums and tapping on coconut shells with a short stick. The music was often combined with the chanting of mele, which usually told a story while the dance depicted the actions or concepts of the story. The hula was performed by both men and women. Today's hulas are only a remnant of what was once a very complex and sacred repertoire, though contemporary hula troupes are recreating much of the ancient vigor and variety. Men's hulas, once fallen virtually into disuse, have staged a strong comeback. [Hawai'i State Archives]

Hula

Note the musicians in this engraving. Behind the 'ōlapa, the dancers, sat the ho'opa'a, the supporters, who chanted, sang, and played instruments. Hawaiian musical instruments used for hula included gourd drums, bamboo nose flutes, wooden drums with sharkskin heads, feather-decorated gourd rattles, smooth stones used as castanets, bamboo rattles, and sticks used for beating time. Hawaiians also used small gourd whistles, which were unique to the Islands. Conch shell trumpets, used extensively on occasions of high ceremony, made a very distinctive and mournful sound that could literally be heard for miles.

In this illustration, the women's hair has been whitened above the forehead by application of a lime paste made of crushed coral, a practice that is still widespread in southern Polynesia and Melanesia today. The short hair shown on the women does not fit our standard image of the South Seas maiden with long raven locks, but it was not at all uncommon in many island groups. In more remote islands of southern Polynesia, married women are often recognized by their shorn hair.

Dancing skirts varied widely. In this portrait, the dancers appear to be wearing tapa cloth wraparounds with complicated knots and bows. The "grass" skirt used often in nightclub and movie presentations is not authentically Hawaiian. This particular costume was introduced to Hawai'i by Gilbert Islanders many decades after the scene depicted above. [Bake–Van Dyke Collection]

Captain Cook

Many sea historians believe that Captain James Cook was the greatest seafaring explorer of all time. Born the son of a laborer, he went to sea as an apprentice on a collier in the difficult waters of the North Sea. A competent and cautious navigator, he was painstaking in his calculations and sought constantly to improve his education. He was promoted to mate at age twenty-four and was in line to become captain of his own collier. However, upon the outbreak of war with France, he joined the British Navy as an able-bodied seaman. In those days, officers were chosen more for their powerful connections than for their competence. But Cook was an excellent seaman, and soon rose to positions of command.

Between 1768 and 1779, Cook commanded three exploring expeditions in the Pacific: from Antarctica to Alaska, Kamchatka to New Zealand, and to South America. He discovered scores of island groups, surveyed the unknown New Zealand coast, and proved the non-existence of a hypothetical large continent in the South Pacific.

He came upon Hawai'i while en route to the North Pacific in search of the Northwest Passage. Cook was intelligent and humane. Whenever possible, he attempted peaceful contact with native populations, even attempting (albeit unsuccessfully) to prevent sexual contact between his men and susceptible island people. Not only was Cook a great navigator, he was also a precursor of anthropologists, collecting artifacts and recording the peoples, the ways of life, and the flora and fauna of newfound lands. He was the first sea captain to prevent scurvy among his crew by insisting on a daily ration of sauerkraut for all hands.

His sweeping searches of the vast Pacific left small blanks to be filled in by later explorers. Captain James Cook was fifty years old when struck down at Kealakekua in the Hawaiian Islands. Today, he might be considered in the prime of life, but by the standards of his harsh and short-lived age, he was an old man.

The Resolution and the Discovery, ships of Cook's third voyage, lie at anchor in Kealakekua Bay. Canoes full of curious Hawaiians paddle out to inspect and their strange, pale-complexioned crew. [Hawai'i State Archives]

Captain Cook is deservedly honored for his accomplishments as a navigator and explorer. Strangely, for so famous a man, little is known of his personal life. He was content to let his accomplishments speak for themselves. His journals objectively comment on everything that he saw, yet provide little inkling of the deepest thoughts and character of the man himself. [Hawai'i State Archives]

Captain Cook

[Hawai'i State Archives]

On January 16, 1779, Captain Cook's expedition sailed into the sheltering bay of Kealakekua (The Road of the God) on the west coast of the Big Island of Hawai'i. The harbor was first explored by Cook's sailing master, a man named Bligh, of later *Mutiny on the Bounty* fame. Cook was unaware that the bay featured in the legends of Lono, the hero-god who long ago had departed Hawai'i, promising to return some day. Furthermore, January was the time of the Makahiki, a festival in honor of Lono. The sails of the ships resembled the image of Lono, so many Hawaiians assumed that the god had returned, true to his ancient promise.

In the engraving, Webber depicts what he and the rest of the expedition considered merely an especially fine welcome for their Captain, little realizing how great an homage was taking place. The priests of Lono seem to have received Cook as Lono returned. In Lono's own heiau, Hikiau, they draped the bemused Cook with sacred red tapa cloth, praised him with sacred chants, and offered him consecrated pig.

As seen in this engraving and others, the European artists of the time had a tendency toward depicting the Hawaiians as somewhat idealized European types with darker complexions. Additionally, in crowd scenes, the same face is seen on every Hawaiian portrayed, perhaps a time-saving device on the part of the artist.

Captain Cook and his marines moments before Cook was killed at Kealakekua Bay in 1779. The unfortunate dispute arose over a stolen cutter and the consequences were deeply regretted by both English and Hawaiians once their passions had subsided. [Hawai'i State Archives]

The romance did not last. The Hawaiians welcomed Cook as the god Lono and must certainly have considered his sailors and marines worthy of deference and respect as personal servants of the god. But the personnel of Cook's expedition were all too human, and the Hawaiians were alert and intelligent. The material superiority of the English was the only essential difference between the two peoples. In all other respects they shared the strengths and weaknesses universal to the human condition.

Of all the explorers of that day, Cook was undoubtedly the most humane and thoughtful. In contrast to the brutal standard of treatment common during his time, he took care to assure the health and happiness of his crew. He also made every effort to obtain peaceful contact with newly encountered people, to show them the respect of equals, and to observe and report on them as accurately as possible.

The generosity of King Kalani'ōpu'u (king of the island of Hawai'i and part of Maui) in provisioning the expedition's ships soon exhausted the produce of the region. The sailors, with their constant demands for food and women, tried the patience of the hospitable Hawaiians and, inevitably, disagreements and provocations arose. Many Hawaiians who had thought Cook divine began to wonder if Cook was a mere human.

When the expedition left Kealakekua on February 4, 1779, the weary Hawaiian hosts were much relieved to see what they hoped to be the last of their visitors. Unfortunately, storm gales damaged the *Resolution*'s foremast and the expedition returned for repairs. The *Discovery*'s cutter was stolen on the night of February 13. Cook and nine marines went ashore and attempted to lure Kalani'ōpu'u aboard Cook's flagship as hostage for the cutter. Meanwhile, because of the theft, the British had blockaded exit from the harbor.

They fired on a canoe attempting to leave the harbor and the outraged Hawaiians counterattacked furiously. Four marines and Cook himself were killed, mute testimony to the great explorer's mortality. Today, a monument marks the spot where Cook was struck down on the shore of Kealakekua. There is no monument in memory of the Hawaiians who were killed in this bloody conclusion to Hawai'i's first contact with Europeans.

Queen Lili'uokalani was a prolific composer whose hundreds of songs were sold in sheet music around the world. Perhaps her most famous composition was "Aloha 'Oe," written in 1878. But, her most haunting melody is "Prayer and Serenade," also known as "The Queen's Prayer," composed in 1895 during her eight-month incarceration in 'Iolani Palace, in which she asks forgiveness for those who imprisoned her. [Baker–Van Dyke Collection]

The chief and chiefess Boki and Liliha were among the missionaries' outspoken critics, although Boki initially supported them. The handsome couple accompanied Kamehameha II and Queen Kamāmalu to London in 1824, where this portrait was painted by John Hayter. Boki perished during an 1829 South Pacific sandalwood expedition. In 1831, Liliha helped foment a brief, failed rebellion against the government of Queen Ka'ahumanu. [Hawai'i State Archives]

The text of "Hymn of Kamehameha I" was composed in 1874 by King Kalākaua and soon after set to music by Captain Berger of the Royal Hawaiian Band. It eventually became "Hawai'i Pono-i" and is considered Hawai'i's national anthem. [Baker–Van Dyke Collection]

Princess Ruth Ke'elikōlani was photographed with ali'i Samuel Parker and John Cummins (1877). The half-sister of Kamehameha IV and Kamehameha V, she inherited all the Kamehameha lands after the deaths of her brothers. Her heir was Princess Bernice Pauahi Bishop, the last of the direct descendants of the great conqueror, who established the Bishop Estate. [Hawai'i State Archives]

MONARCHY: THE HAWAIIAN KINGDOM

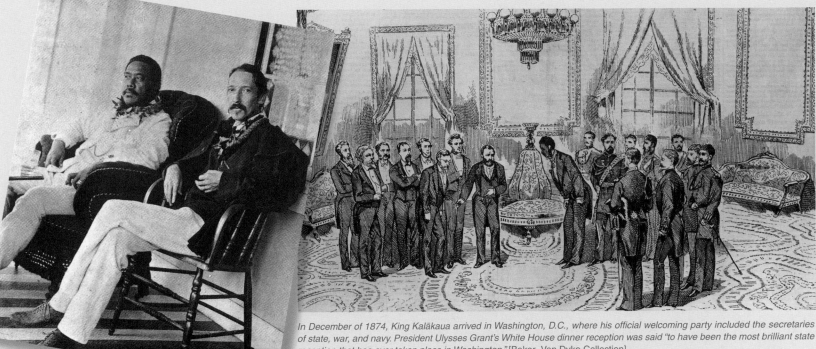

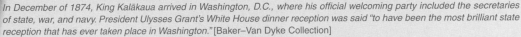

In December of 1874, King Kalākaua arrived in Washington, D.C., where his official welcoming party included the secretaries of state, war, and navy. President Ulysses Grant's White House dinner reception was said "to have been the most brilliant state reception that has ever taken place in Washington." [Baker–Van Dyke Collection]

Kalākaua enjoyed entertaining friends and visitors like Robert Louis Stevenson at his Honolulu Harbor boathouse far from the watchful eyes of the missionaries. [Hawai'i State Archives]

During the 1850s, whaling fleets replenished their supplies and pursued licentious pleasures in the many saloons of Nu'uanu Avenue. When trouble broke out, which was frequently, troops from nearby Honolulu Fort quelled the rioting. With the construction of the Bethel police station and O'ahu Prison, the Fort's usefulness ended and it was demolished in 1857. [Hawai'i State Archives]

Kamehameha I

Born circa 1753 - 1758, Died 1819

King Kamehameha was born in the Hawaiian stone age, a virtually timeless epoch in which the technology of one century differed little, if at all, from that of previous centuries. Yet by the time of Kamehameha's death, Hawai'i's native culture and neolithic technology were on the verge of extinction. His fledgling kingdom was in the throes of what is today known as "future shock." Each day brought new wonders, new problems, new opportunities, and new disappointments.

His birthplace was the Kohala region, northernmost corner of the island of Hawai'i. No one knows, nor may ever know, the exact year of his birth, but most experts think that it was some time in the 1750s. As a young man of about twenty-five, he was present at Kealakekua when Captain Cook's ships anchored there.

The young future king was the nephew of Kalani'ōpu'u, king of the island of Hawai'i (and the Hāna district of eastern Maui). At the time of Cook's visit, each of the major islands was ruled by a separate king. Various kings in Hawaiian history had attempted, without success, to unite the entire island chain under one command.

In 1780, sickly and sensing that death was near, Kamehameha's aged uncle, King Kalani'ōpu'u, named his oldest son, Kīwala'ō, as successor. At the same time Kalani'ōpu'u bestowed a high honor on his nephew Kamehameha, selecting him to be the custodian of Kūkā'ilimoku, the war god. However exalted this honor, Kamehameha was ambitious for higher powers. He traveled to Kohala where he kept a wary eye on developments until his uncle's death.

When Kalani'ōpu'u died, Kamehameha made his move to gain control. The deciding battle was fought at Moku'ōhai, where Kīwala'ō was slain. Kamehameha then proceeded to establish his rule over the entire island of Hawai'i. With the Big Island safely in hand, he set out to conquer the leeward islands, obtaining Maui, Lāna'i, and Moloka'i.

To take O'ahu, he built an immense fleet of canoes. They landed in a two-pronged attack, with half the fleet coming ashore at Wai'alae and half at Waikīkī. The united force drove O'ahu's defenders into Nu'uanu Valley, where their defense became a desperate last stand. Trapped in the valley, the O'ahuans were forced to surrender or be pushed over the steep Nu'uanu Pali.

The conquest of O'ahu effectively established the bold and brilliant warrior as king of all Hawai'i. (Recognizing the inevitable, the king of Kaua'i and Ni'ihau accepted Kamehameha as his sovereign.) Kamehameha proved equally able as a statesman. He united a nation that had never before been united, and he kept it together in the face of disruptive foreign and domestic elements.

During Kamehameha's reign Hawai'i underwent incredible changes, with the ancient way of life suffering near lethal blows. Foreign ships arrived in increasing numbers, bringing domestic animals, trees, fruits, and plants never before seen in Hawai'i. They also brought venereal and other diseases, alcohol, and firearms, and carried young men away on their sailing ships. With little immunity to new diseases, Hawaiians began to die in alarming numbers, and the destruction of their traditional way of life triggered a loss of will to live.

Kamehameha was an old-style autocrat and democracy was foreign to his philosophy. He was equally conservative in religious matters and maintained all the rites, ceremonies, and kapus inviolate. Though the common people began to question their own religion as a result of foreign influence, they dared not disrespect their traditional gods while Kamehameha lived.

Kamehameha brought Hawai'i into the modern world as a nation preparing to deal with other nations. From a series of petty and forever-warring chiefdoms, he built a nation. The end of his reign was characterized by long years of peace, a stability previously unknown. For this accomplishment alone, he deserves the title history has bestowed upon him, Kamehameha the Great.

(Opposite) Tamaahamaah, King of Sandwich Islands, *is one of the few renderings of the great unifier of Hawai'i actually completed during his lifetime. Dressed in the bright red vest, white shirt, and cravat of Western fashion, Kamehameha was said to have favored this oil painting by an anonymous artist. Although a strong traditionalist and devoted to the ancient religion, he was also a shrewd negotiator who forced the growing number of foreign merchants to trade costly goods like furniture, ships, clothing, and weapons for the sweet-scented ili'ahi, or sandalwood, of the Islands.* [Hawai'i State Archives]

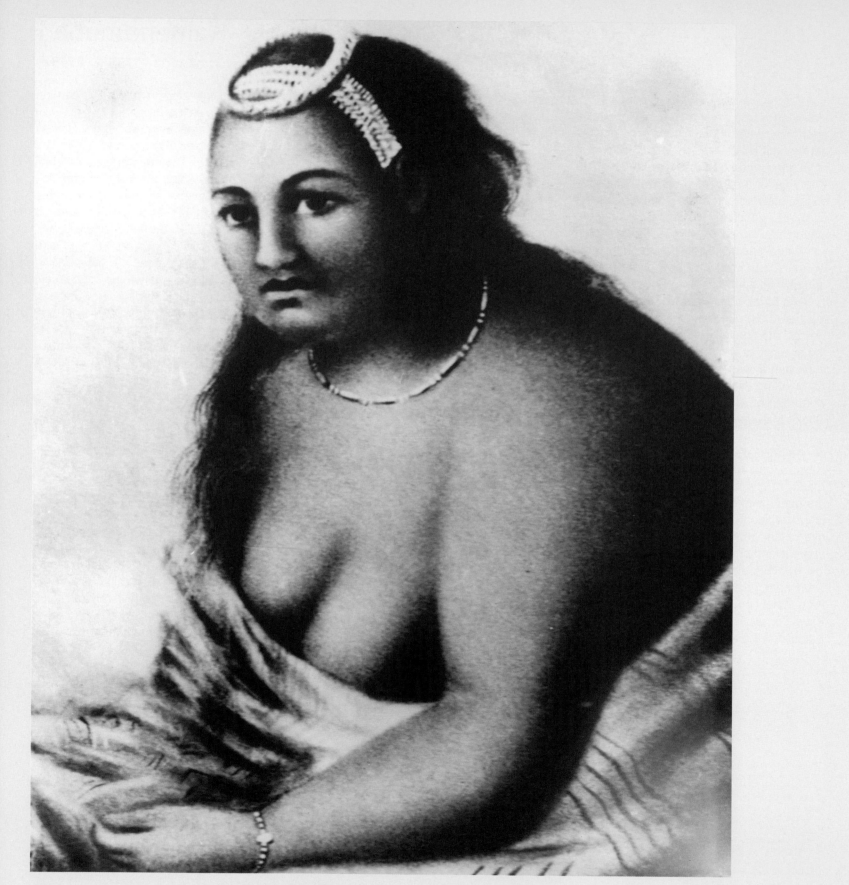

18

Ka'ahumanu

Born 1772, Died 1832

Queen Ka'ahumanu was an unusual woman for her time and place. Were she alive today, it is very likely that she would still be considered highly unorthodox. She played a powerful role in the lives of Hawai'i's first three kings and, by her actions, several times decided the course of Hawaiian history.

Ka'ahumanu was a complex person endowed with intelligence, wit, audacity, and a powerful ambition. She epitomized the old Hawaiian ideal of beauty, where being large was a sign of prosperity and health. This was particularly true of women in the ali'i class, whose diets helped increase their generous proportions.

Ka'ahumanu was the favorite among Kamehameha I's five acknowledged wives. But she was always a strong-willed woman and her relationship with him was tempestuous. She openly had affairs with other men even after the king, in desperation, had declared a kapu on her body. Death was the penalty for violation of the kapu and at least one chieftain paid with his life for the pleasures of dalliance with the king's wife. At one time, she was very much attracted to another handsome young chief, Kaiana, and when Kamehameha found out about it he was furious. Ka'ahumanu fled to the home of her parents fearing that the king would beat her violently. Kamehameha loved her but was too proud to ask her to return home. Captain George Vancouver of the British Navy, a good friend of the king, served as a go-between and skillfully arranged the couple's reconciliation.

Ka'ahumanu bore no children to Kamehameha the Great, but nevertheless managed to dominate two of his sons who successively became kings after his death. At the accession of Kamehameha II, she boldly appropriated half of the new king's power and became the first kuhina nui, or premier, an office that was held only by women until it was abolished in 1866. She was primarily responsible for the overthrow of the kapu system. In league with the king's mother, Ke'ōpuolani, she convinced Kamehameha II to sit down and eat with them, in violation of one of ancient Hawai'i's most serious prohibitions.

As a politically ambitious woman, it was in her interest to defy the kapu system, however great the risk. In old Hawai'i women were second-class citizens, more severely handicapped by the kapu system than the men of any class. They were forbidden to eat many delicious foods, they could not eat with their men, and so on. With the overthrow of the kapu system, Ka'ahumanu was free to exercise her political authority.

When Christian missionaries arrived in 1820, she was cool toward them at first. Later she became a champion of Protestantism, so much so that she expelled French Catholic missionaries and severely strained Hawai'i's relations with France.

Though Kamehameha the Great had united the kingdom, Kaua'i was still semi-independent under a vassal king. Ka'ahumanu finally consolidated the kingdom by enticing King Kaumuali'i of Kaua'i aboard her ship and then sailing off to Honolulu with him. She not only married Kaumuali'i but also later married his handsome son. Kaua'i was left with no legal contenders for its throne and Ka'ahumanu installed her own man as governor.

In 1823, Kamehameha II and Queen Kamāmalu died while visiting London, and young Kauikeaouli became King Kamehameha III. Ka'ahumanu served as regent until he reached manhood and continued in her office as kuhina nui. Thus, for a time, she was Hawai'i's true ruler. Kamehameha III strongly disagreed with her on the need for new laws and the stricter enforcement of existing ones. Where Ka'ahumanu had become rigidly moralistic, he was increasingly tolerant of the prevailing lawlessness and laxity of morals. Eventually the stubborn kuhina nui had her way and some order was restored to the community.

As she grew older, Ka'ahumanu became more religious, to the point of zealousness and intolerance. She kept Hawai'i Protestant while she lived and other sects of Christianity prospered only after her death. She died in 1832, a remarkable woman by any standard and a great woman in the history of Hawai'i.

(Opposite) Queen Ka'ahumanu, favorite wife of Kamehameha the Great. A bold and intelligent woman, she served as kuhina nui (premier) for Kamehameha II and as regent for Kamehameha III. She played a leading role in the overthrow of the ancient kapu system. When the missionaries arrived in Hawai'i, they realized that efforts to convert a nation without the support of chiefs and chiefesses would be futile. King Kamehmeha II had little interest in Christianity, as did his wife, Queen Kamāmalu. Attempts to proselytize often fell on deaf ears. Queen Ka'ahumau originally rejected the religious zeal of Reverend Bingham, making the unofficial head of the mission bow and touch the tip of her finger in great deference. Then in 1825, a nearly fatal illness, followed by a full recovery, led to her conversion—a spiritual transformation. [Hawai'i State Archives]

Kamehameha II

Born 1797, Died 1824

It is hard to imagine a greater contrast in character than the one between young Liholiho (Kamehameha II) and his father, Kamehameha I. Where the Great King had been firm, his son wavered; where the father was strong, the son was weak.

Liholiho was twenty-two years old when he became king at Kailua-Kona on May 20, 1819. He had barely been sworn in when Ka'ahumanu, his father's favored wife, confronted him in front of the assembled nobles and said that it had been his father's wish for her to share rulership of the land. Had anyone attempted such audacity in front of Kamehameha I, the culprit might well have been slain on the spot. Liholiho, offering no objection, split his power in half by accepting Ka'ahumanu as kuhina nui, a newly invented title meaning premier, but which implied the sharing of kingly power.

Always unsure of his power, the fledgling king allowed a further dissipation of kingly prerogative by submitting to the demand of the chiefs that the royal sandalwood monopoly be turned over to them.

Early in Liholiho's reign an event of major proportions within the context of traditional Hawaiian society took place. It was preceded by incessant pressures on the king initiated by Ka'ahumanu and Ke'ōpuolani, his mother. One day at a feast in Kailua, and after much hesitation and deliberation, Liholiho sat down to eat with a group of noble women in view of onlooking commoners. It was a serious matter, for his power and that of the ali'i was bolstered by the kapu system. Yet by openly violating one of the most sacred of all kapus, that which prohibited men and women from eating together, he helped prove that the ancient religion of Hawai'i was valueless. Shortly thereafter, Liholiho ordered god images burned and heiaus demolished throughout the Islands. The ancient social fabric was rent beyond repair.

Kamehameha II was a restless man, constantly fleeing from the problems and responsibilities of his office. It was a time of great changes and he was unable to cope with them. It was inevitable that a man of his nature would venture beyond Hawai'i.

On November 27, 1823, Kamehameha II boarded a chartered ship along with his queen, Kamāmalu, and a few chiefs and women, and sailed to England. The Hawaiian entourage toured London, attended the theater, and joined the merriment at parties and entertainments arranged in their honor by the British aristocracy. A formal audience with King George IV had to be cancelled when both the king and queen contracted measles, a disease to which the Hawaiians had no immunity. Queen Kamāmalu died on July 8, 1824, and the despondent King Kamehameha II followed her on July 14. Their bodies were returned to Hawai'i aboard HMS *Blonde* of the British Navy, commanded by Captain Lord Byron, cousin of the famed poet.

During the reign of Kamehameha II (Liholiho), the ancient kapu system was overthrown, the American missionaries arrived, and the sandalwood trade flourished. Liholiho also led a stormy voyage to Kaua'i to bring back as his vassal Kaumuali'i, that island's king. [Hawai'i State Archives]

Kamehameha III

Born 1814, Died 1854

Kauikeaouli, the last son of Kamehameha the Great to rule, ascended the throne of Hawai'i when he was ten years old, upon the death of his older brother Liholiho (King Kamehameha II) in London. Kuhina nui Ka'ahumanu governed as regent during Kauikeaouli's boyhood with the assistance of a council of chiefly advisors. His reign of twenty-nine years was the longest of any Hawaiian monarch.

Kauikeaouli was king at a most difficult period in Hawai'i's history. The influx of large numbers of foreign residents brought new problems concerning trade, credit, land titles, and a plague of complications unknown to the simple Hawai'i of just a few generations earlier. At a time when traditional Hawaiian social restraints had broken down, the prevailing lawlessness provoked tensions with foreign countries, particularly Great Britain.

Nevertheless, Kamehameha III brought his kingdom safely through a long reign full of difficulties. Although he yearned for a return to old ways, he instituted progressive measures for the good of his people. In his lifetime, Hawai'i moved from autocracy toward democracy and from kingship to constitutional monarchy.

King Kamehameha III died in Honolulu on December 15, 1854, after having named his nephew, Alexander Liholiho, as successor. Kauikeaouli served Hawai'i long and to the best of his ability and conscience. That he was beloved by his people is his epitaph in Hawaiian history.

King Kamehameha III ruled Hawai'i longer than any other monarch and guided the kingdom through a difficult period of transition. The Hawaiians called him Ka Mo'i Lokomaika'i (The Benevolent King). [Hawai'i State Archives]

Kamehameha III

Prince Kauikeaouli

Princess Nahi'ena'ena

During his young manhood, personal troubles worthy of a Greek tragedy embittered his life. Prince Kauikeaouli and his sister, Princess Nahi'ena'ena, were very much in love. Shocking as this may seem to modern Western sensibilities, such unions were acceptable among the nobles of ancient Hawai'i, just as they were among the Egyptian pharaohs. Close relatives often married to keep the chiefly bloodlines pure and to ensure that children would have powerful mana or spiritual power. This word describes a Polynesian concept in which certain persons possess supernatural power and authority derived from their ancestors. Mana is accumulated by uniting persons or families with powerful mana, and offspring of these pure bloodlines were considered even closer to the divine than their parents. The greater the charge of mana, the greater his sacred power, the greater his right to rule. Tortured by love for her brother and guilt from newfound Christian beliefs that had made inroads into traditional Hawaiian ways, Princess Nahi'ena'ena drifted into despondency and died at the age of twenty-one. Long after Prince Kauikeaouli became King Kamehameha III, he regularly visited her grave in Lahaina. [Hawai'i State Archives]

Kamehameha IV

Born 1834, Died 1863

Alexander Liholiho succeeded his uncle, Kamehameha III, on December 15, 1854, taking the title of Kamehameha IV. He was the first grandson of Kamehameha the Great to become King of Hawai'i.

During Kamehameha IV's reign and that of his successor, there was growing agitation on the part of the sugar planters for annexation to the United States to secure a dependable market for their product. At the same time, the Hawaiian monarchs sought to strengthen their own power and carry out a policy of "Hawai'i for the Hawaiians." Within the Hawaiian government there was continuous wrangling between those who were interested in strengthening the power of the throne and those who wished to limit that power and extend democracy to the citizenry. Many foreign residents did not wish to become citizens of Hawai'i but wanted to be able to vote in elections. They wanted political power to safeguard their interests and would have preferred that common Hawaiians remain voteless.

When Alexander was still a fifteen-year-old prince, Finance Minister Gerrit Judd took him and his brother, Lot, on a European trip designed to further their education as future monarchs and to settle some differences that had soured relations between France and the Hawaiian Kingdom. While in France, the young princes were entertained by the highest elements of society and met with Emperor Louis Napoleon.

In 1856, Kamehameha IV married the beautiful Emma Rooke, a part-European descendant of Hawaiian chieftains and granddaughter of an Englishman. A cultivated and witty pair, Alexander and Emma came to symbolize all that was elegant, stylish, and artistic. Though they brought many non-Hawaiian advisors into the government, they were careful to limit missionary participation. King Kamehameha IV was one of the most anti-American of all Hawai'i's monarchs and he showed a marked preference for the British from an early age.

The royal pair became the proud parents of Prince Albert, a bright and handsome little boy who was the apple of their eye and the hope of the Kamehameha dynasty. Unfortunately, tiny Prince Albert died when only four years old and the king never recovered from this shattering blow to his love and hopes. Fifteen months later, on November 30, 1863, Alexander Liholiho died. After his death, Queen Emma attempted once more to become a monarch. In 1874, her candidacy for queen was considered by the Hawaiian Legislature but David Kalākaua was elected.

As a young prince during his visit to New York City, Kamemehameha IV was mistaken for a servant by a railway conductor and ordered out of the car. His anger at racial discrimination was deepened by his fear that Hawai'i might be taken over by the United States as part of its manifest destiny policy. He gradually swung away from using Americans as his advisors, seeking to revive British influence in the kingdom. [Hawai'i State Archives]

Kamehameha V

Born 1830, Died 1872

Lot Kamehameha, as King Kamehameha V, was the final direct descendant of Kamehameha the Great to sit on Hawai'i's throne and the last Hawaiian monarch to reign in the old style. After him, Hawai'i's rulers were elected by the Hawaiian Legislature—a progressive step for those of a democratic frame of mind but anathema to aristocratic believers in the "divine right" of kings.

Lot was a true descendant of Kamehameha I in more ways than one. Throughout his reign Kamehameha V opposed any erosion of royal power and he oversaw the adoption of a new constitution designed to strengthen the royal hand. He was a more truly Hawaiian king than his younger brother Alexander (Kamehameha IV). While Alexander had been worldly and witty, graceful and elegant, Lot was stolid, and more of a nativist in every respect.

Problems with the United States continued, vexatious as they had been during his brother's reign. Agitation by certain elements in favor of annexation by the U.S. threatened Hawai'i's independence. The king, in an effort to defuse relations between the two countries, promoted a treaty of reciprocity that would allow Hawaiian sugar to enter the American market duty-free. The Civil War had cut the Union off from Southern sugar and so there was a great demand from the North for sugar. Until this time, Hawai'i had depended heavily on the whaling fleets as a source of income. By the end of the 1850s whaling was in a gradual decline and was no longer a strong economic force in the Islands

Racial troubles increased in Lot's era due to well-founded suspicions that the whites were trying to take over the kingdom. In 1866, a fist-fight broke out in the Legislature between white and Hawaiian members. It was a racially divided legislature: white legislators refused to speak Hawaiian, the kingdom's official language, and Native Hawaiian members refused to speak English.

King Lot Kamehameha was in bad health for several years before his death. For some unknown reason, he never discussed the matter of succession, though it was of vital importance since he had never married and had no children. As he lay on his deathbed, his counselors and advisors mentioned at least five eminently eligible candidates, all of them high-ranking ali'i men and women. Lot died on December 1, 1872, his forty-second birthday, without naming a successor, thus ending the dynasty founded by Kamehameha the Great. From then on, Hawai'i's monarchs would be elected.

Lot has been called "the last great chief" of the olden type. He favored a stronger monarchy that almost verged on despotism although he was personally concerned for the welfare of his subjects. [Hawai'i State Archives]

Lunalilo

Born 1835, Died 1874

William Lunalilo was confirmed as King of Hawai'i by the Hawaiian Legislature after an informal popular vote. He took his oath of office at Kawaiaha'o Church on January 12, 1873.

Only two of the five possible candidates for the monarchy campaigned seriously—David Kalākaua, chieftain from a line distantly related to the Kamehamehas, and William Charles Lunalilo, descended from one of the half-brothers of Kamehameha the Great. Although Lunalilo won, Kalākaua was soon to take over because King Lunalilo ascended the throne with an advanced tubercular affliction.

Lunalilo was a man with a taste for music, literature, and the arts. He was known as a drinker, though among the common Hawaiian people his "weakness" was hardly considered worthy of comment. They loved him and would have forgiven him for far worse than a penchant for alcohol.

Lunalilo was more liberal than his predecessor, and made serious efforts to democratize the constitution. Once again, during his short reign, the question of a treaty of reciprocity with the U.S. arose. The Hawaiian sugar industry needed a natural market like the United States to absorb its increasing production. This time, the question of the treaty was linked with the suggestion of ceding Pearl Harbor to the United States in exchange for favorable terms.

Even though he felt it was an unwise accommodation to the powerful American giant, King Lunalilo endorsed the cession. When the news reached the Hawaiian public, they were outraged. They understood that a treaty of reciprocity could be of economic benefit to the kingdom, but objected to the cession of their land to a foreign power. Widespread disapproval of the idea forced its eventual abandonment.

One of the most humiliating events of Lunalilo's short reign was the mutiny of the Royal Household Troops, a small body of Hawaiian soldiers who had long served as the monarchy's standing army. Under Lunalilo's reign the troops struggled under the excessively harsh discipline of the senior officers who ironically, were white foreigners. A mutiny was barely prevented by a plea from the king, who guaranteed amnesty for all participants.

It was a difficult and embarrassing moment that demonstrated all too clearly the downward trajectory of Hawai'i's monarchy. Soon after, the Royal Household Troops were disbanded and the kingdom was left without a standing army, a factor which later helped contribute to the success of those who overthrew the monarchy.

King Lunalilo died on February 3, 1874. His reign had lasted only slightly more than a year. Like his predecessor, he failed to name a successor and the question would be decided by the incoming Legislature of 1874.

Above: King Lunalilo had the distinction of being the first Hawaiian monarch to bequeath his property for charity. He established a home "for the use and accommodation of poor, destitute, and infirm people of Hawaiian blood or extraction, giving preference to old people." [Hawai'i State Archives]

Left: The first Lunalilo Home was constructed in Makiki at a site now occupied by Roosevelt High School. It opened its doors on March 30, 1883. Forty years later, in 1923, the old home was demolished and its elderly residents moved to the second Lunalilo Home in Maunalua Valley, now known as Hawai'i Kai. [Baker–Van Dyke Collection]

Kalākaua

Born 1836, Died 1891

In 1874, the newly elected King Kalakaua departed for the United States, a journey that proved indispensable for the success of the reciprocity treaty. President Grant lent his full support, and final approval by both governments came in August of 1876. The treaty allowed Hawaiian crude sugar to be imported duty-free into the U.S. The treaty intricately bound the economy of the Islands to America; American capital, technology, and management tightened their control over Hawai'i. This photograph was taken at the White House. [Hawai'i State Archives]

King David Kalākaua was elected by the Hawaiian Legislature of 1874 amid scenes of violence and indignity. His rival for the throne was the dowager Queen Emma. What her followers lacked in numbers they supplied in willingness to make trouble.

Kalākaua was concerned for the well-being of his Native Hawaiian people. He maintained a policy of filling administrative posts with Hawaiians wherever possible, a practice that caused fear in American businessmen who had supported him

against Queen Emma, hoping to gain power in government. Still, Kalākaua repeatedly and sincerely insisted that there was room in Hawai'i for all kinds of people.

The new king soon proved himself a hard-headed, unpredictable individualist. He fired cabinet members and ministers when they disagreed with him. He envisioned himself as a Polynesian emperor, dreaming of a Federation of Pacific Islands with Hawai'i at its head and himself at the helm. He meddled in the affairs of Samoa, going so far as to obtain the signature of the Samoan King (Malietoa) on an agreement of federation, at a time when Samoa was fending off German, American, and British imperialists.

In late 1882, when the new 'Iolani Palace was completed, Kalākaua decided that such a magnificent stage deserved an equally magnificent performance. On February 12, 1883, he held a coronation ceremony during which he crowned himself king in the manner of Napoleon. Though much of the ceremony was borrowed from European protocol, Kalākaua attempted to blend it with Hawaiian traditions, including dancing of the ancient sacred hulas.

King Kalākaua became known in Hawaiian history as the "Merry Monarch." He loved parties, balls, and entertainments, and was quick to make friends with noted visitors such as Robert Louis Stevenson.

Toward the end of his reign, Kalākaua suffered various setbacks to his power. His cabinet was overthrown, a new constitution that deprived him of almost all his power was written, and in July 1889, an ill-fated insurrection, favoring the abdication of Kalākaua and his replacement by Princess Lili'uokalani, took place. In November 1890, Kalākaua traveled to San Francisco, California, in declining health, leaving Lili'uokalani as regent in his stead. He suffered a stroke and died in San Francisco on January 20, 1891, at the age of fifty four.

'Iolani Palace

Little imagination is required to picture the last home of Hawai'i's monarchs, 'Iolani Palace, filled with nobles, ministers, and officials, all dressed in fancy uniforms, attending gala balls, and accompanied by beautiful ladies in elegant gowns. 'Iolani means "Royal Hawk." The hawk, which flies high above other birds, was a symbol of royalty.

The present rococo and gingerbread fairytale building is actually the second 'Iolani Palace to stand on the site. The first, a much less impressive cottage-like structure, was constructed in 1845. Its first occupant was King Kamehameha III. By the time King David Kalākaua ascended the throne, the old palace was no longer considered a fitting residence for a king and it was torn down to be replaced by the present 'Iolani Palace.

'Iolani Palace was the crowning achievement of King Kalākaua's "new departure in Hawaiian politics." The cornerstone of the structure described as "American Renaissance" was laid in 1879 on Queen Kapi'olani's birthday. Since the king was a member of the Masonic Order, its secret rituals were incorporated into the elaborate ceremony. Three years later, the completed palace was inaugurated with a formal banquet for the Masonic fraternity. The official coronation of King Kalākaua took place on February 12, 1883, at the Coronation Pavilion erected in front of the palace. In this view from the tower of Ali'iolani Hale, the wooden bungalow called Kīna'u Hale is visible just to the left of 'Iolani Palace. Here the king and queen spent a great deal of time, as they preferred its informality and comfort. [Hawai'i State Archives]

The present 'Iolani Palace was completed in 1882; it is constructed of brick, cement and concrete block. Its architecture was a composite of several styles designed to capture the aspirations of the Hawaiian monarchy in the late 1800s.

The palace did not serve long as a residence for royalty. Eleven years after its completion, the monarchy was overthrown and replaced by a provisional government that preceded the Republic of Hawai'i and its later annexation to the United States. Here, Queen Lili'uokalani was held for nine

months as a political prisoner, during which time she wrote many of the lovely songs that are still sung today.

After annexation, 'Iolani Palace remained the center of Hawaiian government under the Territory. The State Senate met in the former royal dining room and the throne room seated the House of Representatives. This situation continued until the completion of a new State Capitol in 1968. 'Iolani Palace has undergone a complete renovation to restore its original splendor.

In 1897, four years after being deposed, Lili'uokalani took her cause before the American people in a journey to Washington, D.C., and New York. This photograph was taken just before her departure. [Hawai'i State Archives]

Lili'uokalani

Born 1838, Died 1917

Lili'uokalani was already leading the nation as regent when King Kalākaua died in San Francisco. At the time that she became queen, the political and economic climate was extremely complicated. Rivalry was intense between white businessmen who dominated the economy and native politicians who still retained power.

The possibility of annexation to the United States was being openly discussed by a small group of businessmen and wealthy foreigners. Though the annexationists were badly outnumbered, they were not intimidated by lack of popular support. On the whole, these businessmen considered Hawaiians incapable of self-government and believed that the monarchy was too inept to safeguard the interests of property and profits.

Tension grew when the queen announced her intention to promulgate a new constitution which would restore the power of the monarchy, much of which had been lost in 1887 under a constitution signed by King Kalākaua. Even members of her own cabinet were alarmed and disapproving, fearing that it would give the annexationists the ammunition they sought. A Committee of Public Safety was formed by the annexationists. They then created a provisional government and a militia. The queen could have declared martial law and arrested the conspirators, but she felt that this would begin armed conflict and might cost the innocent lives of her people. Under the command of Captain G. C. Wiltse, an open supporter of the provisional government, marines and sailors from the USS *Boston* landed to keep order in Honolulu. A day later, the Committee of Public Safety sent armed companies of militia to take over government buildings and offices. The queen was stripped of power.

She sent a plea to the U.S. minister, asking him to support her sovereignty, but he replied that the provisional government was now the only recognized government in Hawai'i. Just after sunset on January 17, 1893, the queen surrendered under protest. On January 31, Minister Stevens, at the request of the provisional government's advisory council, raised the U.S. flag over Honolulu, believing annexation would soon follow. However, in March 1893 President Cleveland sent a special investigator to Hawai'i with instructions to determine the chain of events that led to the raising of the American flag. After the investigation, President Cleveland's administration concluded that the monarchy had been overthrown by force with the complicity of the U.S. minister.

The provisional government refused to step down. Under Cleveland, the U.S. refused to annex Hawai'i. Yet Lili'uokalani's reign as queen of Hawai'i had ended. The Provisionals, though disheartened by Washington's rejection, boldly established the Republic of Hawai'i on July 4, 1894, making Sanford Dole president.

In 1895, Hawaiians loyal to the queen staged a revolt in an attempt to restore Lili'uokalani to the throne. The revolt was crushed and the queen was placed under house arrest in an apartment of 'Iolani Palace. She also was forced to relinquish any claim to the throne as a condition to obtain amnesty for the Hawaiian rebels.

The Spanish-American War in 1898 precipitated American reconsideration of its position on Hawai'i. The U.S. had taken over the Philippines and Hawai'i's strategic value was now obvious. President McKinley signed the resolution of annexation on July 7, 1898. It may have been a happy day for the businessmen and new ruling classes of Hawai'i, but for many others it was a day of sadness. Large numbers of royalists and common Hawaiians gathered quietly at the home of deposed Queen Lili'uokalani and Crown Princess Ka'iulani to silently console them and pay homage to the last monarch of the lost kingdom. On June 14, 1900, Hawai'i formally became a territory under the Organic Act, and Sanford Dole, who had served as president of the Hawaiian Republic, was sworn in as Hawai'i's first territorial governor.

As a young princess the queen had married John Dominis, who inherited a home located just behind 'Iolani Palace, known as Washington Place. After the overthrow of her government until her death in 1917, Lili'uokalani resided there. She is best known to the outside world as the composer of "Aloha 'Oe," the lovely and haunting song that evokes Hawai'i wherever it is heard.

Though she was legally known as Lydia Dominis after her forced abdication, the people of Hawai'i called her Queen Lili'uokalani as long as she lived, and this remains her name in Hawaiian hearts today.

Overthrow

On June 5, 1900, the Territory of Hawai'i was inaugurated. 'Iolani Palace, renamed the Executive Building, was bedecked with the colorful bunting of "Old Glory." The former kingdom's flag was given a subordinate role as a territorial emblem for the doorway. Thousands of supporters of this new American presence gathered on the Palace grounds to witness Sanford Ballard Dole, former president of the provisional government and the Republic of Hawai'i, take his oath of office as governor of the territory. U.S. troops formed a perimeter around the pro-American crowd. For the majority of Hawaiians loyal to the monarchy, this "glorious day" was one of deep bitterness. At the end of the twentieth century, their descendants would critically examine the historic events leading to annexation, and actively seek restoration of their sovereign rights. [Hawai'i State Archives]

On July 4, 1894, when efforts to annex Hawai'i to the United States were thwarted by President Grover Cleveland and anti-imperialist members of the Democratic Party, the provisional government declared itself the Republic of Hawai'i. Sanford B. Dole was elected president. Six months later, in January of 1895, as its leaders prepared to celebrate the second anniversary of the Hawaiian kingdom's downfall, Robert Wilcox, Samuel Nowlein, and a coalition of Hawaiians and royalist sympathizers attempted to overthrow the republic. Wilcox had intended to land guns at Sans Souci beach on the evening of January 6, 1895. Informers tipped off the sheriff and his deputies. Gunfire broke out on the beach at Waikīkī as the revolutionists broke rank and scattered toward Diamond Head and up into Pālolo and Mānoa valleys. Honolulu was placed under martial law. Wilcox is pictured here in his flamboyant self-designed uniform. The photo was taken after an earlier arrest, in 1889, when he led an uprising against the signing of the "Bayonet" Constitution. [Hawai'i State Archives]

Officers of the Provisional Government of Hawai'i after the overthrow of the monarchy and shortly before the establishment of the short-lived republic which was followed by U.S. annexation. Shown here are (left to right), James A. King, Sanford B. Dole (president of the Republic and first territorial governor), William O. Smith, and Peter C. Jones. [Baker–Van Dyke Collection]

Citizens Guard were used to thwart opposition to the overthrow. [Hawai'i State Archives]

On the evening of January 16, 1893, troops of the USS Boston landed. They were quartered at the Arlington Hotel in downtown Honolulu, the former home of Princess Bernice Pauahi Bishop. The hotel became known as "Camp Boston" when martial law was declared by the provisional government. The 162 soldiers were supposedly put into position only to protect American property and lives during anticipated political upheavals in the kingdom. Queen Lili'uokalani protested that a majority of the troops were quartered directly across from Ali'iolani Hale, the government building almost across from 'Iolani Palace, an area where no Americans resided or owned property. The troops were in an excellent position, however, to defend the leaders of the revolution who were about to declare a provisional government. [Hawai'i State Archives]

Refusing President Grover Cleveland's demand that the Hawai'i Provisional Government return authority to Queen Lili'uokalani, the American businessmen who had overthrown the monarchy formally established the Republic of Hawai'i on July 4, 1894. Their plan was to wait for the election of a president sympathetic to their goal, which occurred in August 1898 when President McKinley declared that Hawai'i would become part of the U.S. [Hawaiian Historical Society]

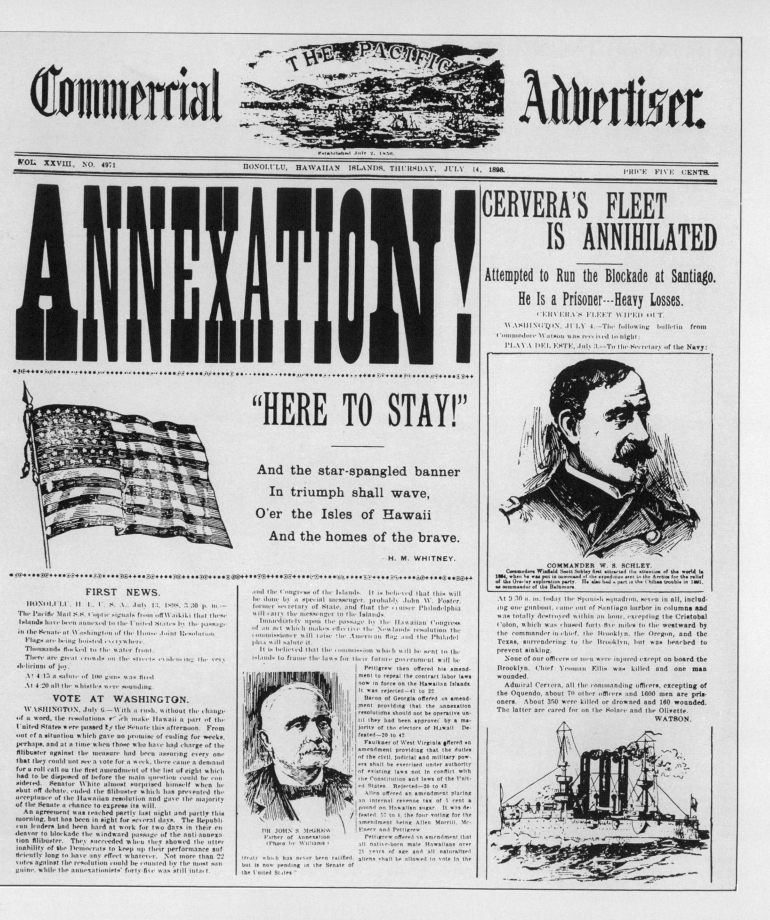

Commercial

THE PACIFIC

Advertiser.

Established July 2, 1856.

VOL. XXVIII., NO. 4971.   HONOLULU, HAWAIIAN ISLANDS, THURSDAY, JULY 14, 1898.   PRICE FIVE CENTS.

ANNEXATION!

"HERE TO STAY!"

And the star-spangled banner
In triumph shall wave,
O'er the Isles of Hawaii
And the homes of the brave.

—H. M. WHITNEY.

CERVERA'S FLEET IS ANNIHILATED

Attempted to Run the Blockade at Santiago.

He Is a Prisoner---Heavy Losses.

CERVERA'S FLEET WIPED OUT.

WASHINGTON, JULY 4.—The following bulletin from Commodore Watson was received to-night:

PLAYA DEL ESTE, July 3.—To the Secretary of the Navy:

COMMANDER W. S. SCHLEY.
Commodore Winfield Scott Schley first attracted the attention of the world in 1884, when he was put in command of the expedition sent to the Arctic for the relief of the Greeley exploration party. He also had a part in the Chilian trouble in 1891, as commander of the Baltimore.

At 9:30 a. m. today the Spanish squadron, seven in all, including one gunboat, came out of Santiago harbor in columns and was totally destroyed within an hour, excepting the Cristobal Colon, which was chased forty five miles to the westward by the commander in-chief, the Brooklyn, the Oregon, and the Texas, surrendering to the Brooklyn, but was beached to prevent sinking.

None of our officers or men were injured except on board the Brooklyn. Chief Yeoman Ellis was killed and one man wounded.

Admiral Cervera, all the commanding officers, excepting of the Oquendo, about 70 other officers and 1600 men are prisoners. About 350 were killed or drowned and 160 wounded. The latter are cared for on the Solace and the Olivette.

WATSON.

FIRST NEWS.

HONOLULU, H. I., U. S. A., July 13, 1898, 3:30 p. m.—The Pacific Mail S.S. Coptic signals from off Waikiki that these Islands have been annexed to the United States by the passage in the Senate at Washington of the House Joint Resolution.

Flags are being hoisted everywhere.

Thousands flocked to the water front.

There are great crowds on the streets evidencing the very delirium of joy.

At 4:15 a salute of 100 guns was fired.

At 4:20 all the whistles were sounding.

VOTE AT WASHINGTON.

WASHINGTON, July 6.—With a rush, without the change of a word, the resolutions which make Hawaii a part of the United States were passed by the Senate this afternoon. From out of a situation which gave no promise of ending for weeks, perhaps, and at a time when those who have had charge of the filibuster against the measure had been assuring every one that they could not see a vote for a week, there came a demand for a roll call on the first amendment of the list of eight which had to be disposed of before the main question could be considered. Senator White almost surprised himself when he shut off debate, ended the filibuster which has prevented the acceptance of the Hawaiian resolution and gave the majority of the Senate a chance to express its will.

An agreement was reached partly last night and partly this morning, but has been in sight for several days. The Republican leaders had been hard at work for two days in their endeavor to blockade the windward passage of the anti-annexation filibuster. They succeeded when they showed the utter inability of the Democrats to keep up their performance sufficiently long to have any effect whatever. Not more than 22 votes against the resolution could be counted by the most sanguine, while the annexationists' forty-five was still intact.

and the Congress of the Islands. It is believed that this will be done by a special messenger, probably John W. Foster, former secretary of State, and that the cruiser Philadelphia will carry the messenger to the Islands.

Immediately upon the passage by the Hawaiian Congress of an act which makes effective the Newlands resolution the commissioner will raise the American flag and the Philadelphia will salute it.

It is believed that the commission which will be sent to the islands to frame the laws for their future government will be

Pettigrew then offered his amendment to repeal the contract labor laws now in force on the Hawaiian Islands. It was rejected—41 to 22.

Bacon of Georgia offered an amendment providing that the annexation resolutions should not be operative until they had been approved by a majority of the electors of Hawaii. Defeated—20 to 42.

Faulkner of West Virginia offered an amendment providing that the duties of the civil, judicial and military powers shall be exercised under authority of existing laws not in conflict with the Constitution and laws of the United States. Rejected—20 to 43.

Allen offered an amendment placing an internal revenue tax of 1 cent a pound on Hawaiian sugar. It was defeated, 57 to 4, the four voting for the amendment being Allen Morrill, McEnery and Pettigrew.

Pettigrew offered an amendment that all native-born male Hawaiians over 21 years of age and all naturalized aliens shall be allowed to vote in the

DR JOHN S. McGREW.
Father of Annexation
(Photo by Williams.)

treaty which has never been ratified, but is now pending in the Senate of the United States."

Reception at Washington Place in honor of Queen Liliʻuokalani's return from Washington, August 2, 1898. Left to right: Prince David Kawānanakoa, Princess Kaʻiulani, Queen Liliʻuokalani, Prince Kūhiō, Mrs. J. O. Carter and her daughter Mrs. Sarah Babbit. [Hawaiian Historical Society]

The Hawaiian police reluctantly take an oath of allegiance to the United States following the annexation ceremonies on August 12, 1898. [Hawaiʻi State Archives]

Princess Ka'iulani

Her story is one of romance and tragedy, the short life of a beautiful princess whose kingdom was stolen from her, whose throne ceased to exist as she was preparing herself to occupy it.

Ka'iulani was born October 16, 1875, to Princess Miriam Likelike and Archibald Cleghorn, a prominent Honolulu businessman from Edinburgh, Scotland. On Christmas Day of the same year, in St. Andrew's Cathedral, she was christened Victoria Kawēkiu Lunalilo Kalaninuiahilapalapa Ka'iulani. A descendant of the highest Hawaiian ali'i, her uncle King David Kalākaua ruled Hawai'i when she was born, and her aunt Lili'uokalani was to become the last queen of Hawai'i. King Kalākaua was particularly overjoyed at her birth. Childless himself, he was happy to know that his sister had produced an heir to the throne to follow Lili'uokalani.

Princess Ka'iulani spent a happy childhood at her family's home in Waikīkī. A beautiful estate surrounded by lush gardens and walkways, it was called 'Āinahau, meaning "cool place" in the Hawaiian language. It seemed an idyllic existence, with the house always full of interesting people, her parents well-liked by Hawaiians and non-Hawaiians alike. Yet the tragedies that were to form Ka'iulani's character began to occur at an early age. Her mother, Princess Likelike, became ill in December 1886. She became increasingly quiet and withdrawn. On the afternoon of February 2, 1887, Likelike died at the age of thirty-seven, leaving behind a distraught husband and an inconsolable twelve-year-old daughter.

After a period of mourning, the family home at 'Āinahau continued to be one of the most popular settings for Honolulu's elite. Perhaps the most interesting visitor of all, especially from the young princess's viewpoint, was Robert Louis Stevenson, who had sailed into Honolulu Harbor in January 1889. He became friends with Kalākaua, who introduced him to Ka'iulani and her father. Stevenson was thoroughly captivated by the beautiful young Scots-Hawaiian princess, and the two spent long hours conversing together under the large banyan tree in front of 'Āinahau.

When Ka'iulani turned thirteen, it was thought she should have an education befitting a future occupant of the Hawaiian throne in this new era. She became the first member of the Hawaiian royalty to receive the kind of training traditionally given to the children of European monarchs in preparation for ascension to the throne.

Princess Ka'iulani sailed to England via San Francisco in 1889, and it would be eight long years before the lovely young woman returned to her native Islands. During her stay in Europe, she traveled widely and was taught French, German, literature, and other subjects, including the social graces expected of one in her high position.

With each passing year her beauty grew and matured and she soon became a very popular young woman, pursued by eligible bachelors from the nobility and upper strata of European society. Though she was a high-spirited and vivacious girl, she never took any of her suitors seriously, concentrating more on preparation for the destiny that awaited her at home.

But news from home became more puzzling and ominous with each passing day, beginning with a letter from her uncle Kalākaua who warned enigmatically that she be on guard against enemies. This was to be the last letter from the king to Ka'iulani. He died in San Francisco on January 20, 1891, while consulting with physicians about his deteriorating health.

The king's sister, Lili'uokalani, next in line for the throne, became the reigning monarch and Ka'iulani was now the crown princess. Lil'iuokalani's reign was short-lived and she had to deal with treachery at every turn, as prominent businessmen and even members of her own cabinet plotted against her.

In January of 1893, Ka'iulani was to hear that the monarchy had been overthrown and that a provisional government had taken power. This bad news had its effect on the vulnerable young princess and her health began to falter. Already homesick, she increasingly felt the urge to return to Hawai'i, where she could help her people.

Princess Ka'iulani journeyed to Washington and sought an audience with President Cleveland to plead the cause of the monarchy against the usurpers of the provisional government (who were at the same time lobbying for annexation by the U.S. government). The gentle and aristocratic bearing of the exotically beautiful princess captivated the American public, which sympathized with her plight. The president appointed a commissioner to investigate the situation in Hawai'i, an action which frustrated the provisionals for many months. Having done what she could, Ka'iulani returned to Europe to resume her studies. She came home to Hawai'i in 1897.

Although the royalist cause was desperate, the fight continued. Hawaiians referred to Ka'iulani as "Our Last Hope." Finally, in 1898, Hawai'i was annexed to the United States and Ka'iulani's right to become queen of her nation was lost for all time.

Ka'iulani went through the motions of living but something seemed to have gone out of her. She still attended the round of lū'aus and parties and outings that were her lot as a popular princess, but her former vitality disappeared. Her attitude became increasingly fatalistic and she seemed to live for nothing.

More and more she sought to escape from Honolulu, with its atmosphere of swaggering American soldiers and the arrogance of the new government. In December 1898, Ka'iulani accepted an invitation to attend a wedding at the Parker Ranch in the cool uplands of the northern part of the Big Island of Hawai'i. She had always loved horseback riding and here she could indulge the pleasure at will. With a defiance that had become part of her character since the downfall of the monarchy and against the advice of her friends, Ka'iulani went riding once too often in the chilly wind and rain. For some time her health had been fragile, and soon she came down with a fever.

Her condition did not improve and she was brought back to Honolulu by ship. In her home at 'Āinahau the doctors diagnosed her condition as rheumatism of the heart complicated by other symptoms. After a lingering illness, Princess Ka'iulani died on March 6, 1899, surrounded by her heartbroken father, friends, and relatives. Thus passed, at only twenty-three years, a beautiful fairytale princess, Hawai'i's "Last Hope." With her death a romantic era faded into the mist of the past. Hawai'i entered the matter-of-fact, coldly realistic twentieth century.

Ka'iulani as a young girl. [Hawai'i State Archives]

As a mature woman Ka'iulani's beauty bewitched all who saw her. The daughter of Governor Archibald Cleghorn and Princess Miriam Likelike, the adored princess died on March 6, 1899, three years after this photo was taken. [Hawai'i State Archives]

Honolulu 1836. [Baker–Van Dyke Collection]

Queen Kīna'u and her ladies return from church near the present site of Kawaiaha'o Church. Circa 1836. [Hawai'i State Archives]

The port of Honolulu in 1857, with the three-story Custom House at the far left. [Hawai'i State Archives]

View of port Hanarourou, 1816. *The spelling was later changed to Honolulu.* [Hawai'i State Archives]

"Society is a queer medley in this notable missionary, whaling and governmental centre," wrote Mr. Twain, commenting on the foreigners he met. *This view of Honolulu Harbor in the 1860s shows churches, government buildings, and saloons where this curious mix of humanity worked and relaxed.* [Hawai'i State Archives]

Asa and Lucy Thurston devoted their entire lives to Mokuʻaikaua Church in Kailua-Kona on the Big Island. They were photographed in Honolulu on their fortieth wedding anniversary in 1859. [Baker–Van Dyke Collection]

OBOOKIAH,
a Native of Owhyhee

Orphaned in Kamehameha's wars of unification, Opukahaia boarded a ship bound for ports around the world. In 1809, he ended up in New Haven where he deeply impressed his New England teachers. In 1816, he attended the Cornwall Mission School, established by the American Board of Commissioners for Foreign Missions to prepare Native American children to return to their people as emissaries of the Christian faith. Opukahaia's memoirs were published under his American name, Henry Obookiah, and translated into many languages. Through his urging the board established a Sandwich Islands Mission. Nearly two centuries later, his remains were returned to Hawaiʻi for reburial. [Hawaiʻi State Archives]

Lorenzo Lyons arrived in Hawaiʻi on May 17, 1832, with the fifth company of missionaries. He spent his life at the Waimea mission station on the Big Island. He composed many beautiful songs in the Hawaiian language, including "Hawaii Aloha." [Hawaiʻi State Archives]

Dr. Gerrit Parmele Judd and Mrs. Laura Fish Judd. [Hawaiʻi State Archives]

Many young Hawaiian chiefs such as Timoteo Haʻalilo (1808– 1844) became world travelers. He accompanied American missionary and government advisor William Richards on a diplomatic mission to the United States, Britain, and France to negotiate treaties respecting the independence of the Islands. While in Paris, Haʻalilo posed for this daguerreotype, believed to be the first known photograph of a Native Hawaiian. The young diplomat never returned to the Islands but succumbed to disease in 1844 on his voyage home. [Baker–Van Dyke Collection]

An anti-missionary adage still current in the Islands says of the missionaries, "They came to do good, and did well." Certainly many missionary descendants used their connections and influence to gain advantages in business and in obtaining large grants of land, but the original missionaries lived spartan lives of dedication, hard work, and self-sacrifice. To them the epigram does a disservice.

Missionaries can hardly be blamed for the destruction of the Hawaiian religion. When they arrived in Hawaiʻi in 1820, prepared to do battle "against the forces of heathenish idolatry," the Hawaiian people had already dismantled their heiaus and had rejected their religious beliefs. One can imagine the surprise with which the missionaries received this unexpected bit of news.

From 1837 to 1840, nearly twenty thousand Hawaiians accepted Christianity. Though they had rejected their own religion a generation earlier, they did not hurry to accept a new one. They observed the detrimental effects of the new foreign influences. The abstract concepts, prohibitions, and demands of Calvinistic Christianity were difficult to understand and practice. But, after observing the good works and unselfishness of the majority of dedicated missionaries, the Hawaiians finally accepted the new religion.

The missionaries who came to Hawaiʻi in the earliest years were from Puritan New England. Naturally, the missionaries varied greatly in individual temperament, character, talent, and training. As a group, their actions seemed morally superior to the motley mixture of tradesmen, adventurers, and riffraff flooding the Islands.

Judged by today's standards, many missionary ideas were extremely narrow and intolerant, but the missionaries did try to do good. They organized the Hawaiian language in written form, enabling the Hawaiian people to record their previously oral culture. They also taught Hawaiians to read and write in their own language. The first mission press printed Bibles, hymnals, textbooks, pamphlets, and periodicals in Hawaiian and English. Schools were established throughout the Islands as rapidly as possible. The missionaries believed strongly in Bible study, and in the importance of literacy. They also taught useful skills such as arithmetic and sewing. By 1831, only eleven years after the missionaries' arrival, some fifty-two thousand pupils had been enrolled.

Missions also encouraged the development of agriculture and manufacturing, which gave Hawaiʻi an economic base to trade with foreign nations. They introduced Western medicine and undertook the kingdom's first modern census.

One more thing must be credited to the missionaries, something that even their detractors admit. They helped Hawaiʻi become and remain an independent nation at a time when Hawaiʻi was ripe for colonization. With their efforts, Hawaiʻi was recognized as a legitimate kingdom governed along modern constitutional lines understood and respected by foreigners as well as Hawaiian citizens. These proselytizers of Christianity were primarily interested in the salvation of souls, yet they were also charged with being an agency of "civilization." In their opinion, one thing was not possible without the other.

It is true that some missionaries "came to do good and did well." But most came only to do good, and did just that.

Youngsters of Kalaupapa. The Hawaiian people were alarmingly susceptible to Hansen's disease, as they were to all diseases brought in from the outside world. [Hawai'i State Archives]

A road in the settlement for people afflicted with Hansen's disease on Moloka'i's Kalawao Peninsula. In the distance, the spectacularly beautiful north Moloka'i coast. [Hawai'i State Archives]

Joseph de Veuster was born on January 3, 1840, in Tremeloo, Belgium, to a family of grain-growing peasants. Always a religious youth, Joseph entered the Sacred Hearts Congregation at Louvain as a postulant in 1859. This first step would take him along the road to beatification as Father Damien, patron of people with Hansen's disease.

In the 1860s, Hawai'i became alarmed at the spread of Hansen's disease, particularly among the Native Hawaiian people. Medical opinion held that the only way to prevent further spread of the disease was to isolate the victims. Thus the Hawaiian Legislature passed the "Act to Prevent the Spread of Leprosy," choosing lonely Kalawao, a peninsula on Moloka'i's north shore, as the place of resettlement. Kalawao was a triangular natural prison surrounded on two sides by rough seas and, at its back, cut off from the rest of the island by steep cliffs. The government planned to furnish farm animals, medical care, and regular shipments of food and other supplies.

In 1866 the first boatload of patients was torn from their weeping relatives and departed from Honolulu en route to Kalawao. Upon arrival, they found that the so-called hospital had no beds, that medicines and doctors were in short supply, and that food shipments were unreliable. Living in sordid conditions and cast out from society, most fell victim to depression and alienation. No attempt whatsoever was made to cure the dread disease.

After completion of his training at Louvain, young Father Damien was assigned to the Sacred Hearts Mission in Hawai'i and was ordained a priest in the Cathedral of Our Lady of Peace in Honolulu on May 21, 1864. On a visit with Bishop Maigret to the settlement, Father Damien was struck with the suffering and almost total abandonment of the victims. He asked the bishop for permission to stay and serve the people, having decided to dedicate his life to the alleviation of their physical and spiritual misery. Bishop Maigret allowed him to remain as long as his devotion continued.

Father Damien's kindly, open nature would not permit anything to come between himself and his beloved charges. He worked alongside them, helped them to obtain better food and warm clothing, to build adequate housing, and to assure a supply of clean, potable water. He built chapels and orphanages—his energy was seemingly boundless.

As the news of his dedication and his work spread throughout the world, funds and help came pouring in. His enthusiastic and loving closeness to the unfortunates exacted its toll and he contracted Hansen's disease, yet he continued to work as long as he was physically able. Eventually his selfless labors were recognized and the government undertook the responsibilities that it had so long avoided.

The Belgian priest died on April 15, 1889. Fellow Hansen's disease sufferers buried him under the tree where he had spent his first nights in the settlement. In 1936, at the request of the Belgian government, his body was returned to the village of his birth.

Today, the tiny settlement of Kalaupapa on Kalawao boasts modern facilities where the remaining patients lead their lives. The affliction is now controllable with drugs and no one is forced to remain at Kalaupapa, but long-time residents consider it home and prefer to stay.

Father Damien de Veuster before he landed in the colony on May 10, 1873. [Hawai'i State Archives]

Left: On June 13, 1992, Pope John Paul II officially approved the "real miracle" attributed to Damien's intercession (Sister Simplicia's overnight cure from a seven-month-long, grave intestinal disease in 1895. She had been praying for a cure through Damien's intercession). On June 4, 1995, Pope John Paul II beatified Father Damien in a Pontifical Mass in Brussels, Belgium, in recognition of a life of extraordinary holiness and heroic virtue. In 2009, Pope Benedict XVI canonized five new saints including Father Damien. This photograph was taken a few weeks before he died in 1889. [Hawai'i State Archives]

Whaling

The whaling industry had an enormous impact on the economy of Hawai'i and dealt a mortal blow to what remained of traditional culture. At its height, hundreds of ships and thousands of seamen crowded the towns of Honolulu and Lahaina as they awaited the seasonal gatherings of their prey in Arctic or Equatorial grounds. The first American whalers moved into the Pacific off Chile in 1791, as whales were becoming more and more scarce in the Atlantic. By 1819 they arrived in Hawai'i, and in 1844 a fleet of 490 whaling ships anchored in Honolulu and off of Lahaina on Maui.

Huge mobs of seamen thronged the towns, spending money "like drunken sailors." Living conditions aboard their ships were brutal, and long dull voyages with no respite ashore left them desperate for good times and excitement. In Hawaiian ports they found women, alcohol, and plenty of trouble. A whaling sailor's idea of fun was diametrically opposed to the standards imposed by missionaries and the local establishment. The result was an almost constant clash with the authorities, all of which imparted a rather lively air to the dockside streets.

It was a case of "you can't live with 'em and you can't live without 'em." Tradesmen and craftsmen of all kinds, from blacksmiths, sundries merchants, and carpenters, to the owners of grog shops and brothels, welcomed the economic stimulus provided by the whaling fleets, while "decent folk" deplored the concurrent scandalous behavior.

Unlike today's whaling ships, which are usually large factory ships with harpoon cannons, the whaling ships of those days required men unafraid to risk their lives. When a whale was sighted, whalers lowered small boats into the water and chased their prey. Once within range of the leviathan, the harpooneer would plunge his weapon into its immense body. Many crews were drowned or smashed to death in the ensuing struggle. In the drawing shown, Hulsart has depicted such a scene as it took place off one of the Hawaiian Islands, probably Maui.

It took boldness and strength to be a whaleman, and many lost their lives when the giant sea mammals smashed the tiny boats of their persecutors. Today the great whales are endangered species, protected by anti-whaling agreements observed by most of the world's nations. The waters between Maui, Moloka'i, and Lāna'i are winter calving grounds for hundreds of whales. These waters were designated and approved as the "Hawaiian Islands Humpback Whale National Marine Sanctuary," making it the nation's twelfth marine sanctuary. [Hawai'i State Archives]

By the end of the nineteenth century, Hawaiians had experienced over one hundred years of contact with Western technology and lifestyles, both of which stood in sharp contrast to their traditional ways. The clash of ideals and values had a disastrous effect on the Hawaiian culture, which suffered amid a flood of new customs, beliefs, and techniques.

First to succumb were the tools, weapons, and utensils that served Hawaiians before contact. Next to suffer was the Hawaiian religion, whose kapu system reflected the importance of preserving the resources of the land and sea. The old religious beliefs lost clout as Hawaiians watched Western intruders violate the most sacred prohibitions of the gods without punishment. In an action perhaps without precedent anywhere on earth, Kamehameha II formally abolished Hawai'i's religion in 1819. Some elements of the old religion, however, survived with surprising strength, particularly the devotion to Pele, the volcano goddess.

With the loss of stability through the loss of the structured Hawaiian religion and the overwhelming impact of new technology, the Hawaiian culture seemed headed toward total extinction. Yet the ancient traditions and philosophy were not as fragile as they first appeared. Hawaiians believed that many of the older beliefs were venerable, useful, and compatible with modern ways; these lifeways should not be abandoned, but passed along to the new Hawai'i. They clung tenaciously to many of their traditions. The idea that all people were of one family, the belief that all problems could be settled by honest discourse, and love and respect for the land, all continued to pervade the spirit of the Islands.

By the late 1800s, when some of the accompanying photographs were taken, many surface aspects of the old Hawaiian way of life were still evident, particularly in remote country areas. Fishermen plied the bays in outrigger canoes and speared their prey at night by torchlight. Whole villages turned out to pull in the giant hukilau fishnets and to share the catch as they had done since anyone could remember. Traditional foods were as popular as ever, were still cooked in the Hawaiian imu or earth oven, and were eaten at old-style lū'au feasts complete with songs and hulas of an earlier time. A few Hawaiians were even living in traditional houses thatched with pili grass. More importantly, much of the ancient spiritual undercurrent ran deep and strong despite more than a century of life in a society increasingly at odds with the basic Hawaiian attitude toward land, nature, and humanity.

The Polynesian attitude toward childraising, the hanai system, was still prevalent. Children were often passed on to relatives or friends who had no children of their own. Hawaiian children grew up in a warm and affectionate world where people not related by blood were considered part of the 'ohana or extended family. To Hawaiians, the family not only consisted of the usual relatives, but included all who were loved or who chose to associate themselves in cooperative actions. Thus, when it seemed to outsiders that a Hawaiian had an unusually large number of relatives, it was only because of unfamiliarity with the Hawaiian concept of family. Another feature of the Hawaiian concept of family was a universal respect for elders.

Another old custom, widely practiced even today, was ho'oponopono, a means of solving conflict through frank discussions designed to restore and maintain good relationships within the family or village group. It included prayer and cultivated respect and the capacity for forgiveness. Hawaiians were not a competitive people. Their greatest strength lay in cooperation through the family or group. This lack of competitive spirit often put them at a disadvantage when dealing with people raised in more ruthless and individualistic traditions.

Overall the Hawaiians felt that life should be happy and enjoyable. It was not necessary to be materially successful. Success was judged more on the basis of how well one was loved and by decency of character. Such attitudes were easier to maintain in the small rural villages than amid the anonymity and alienation of Honolulu. Generosity was also important in the old culture, a quality which was often interpreted as weakness or stupidity by those all too eager to take advantage. It is to their credit that Hawaiians are still known as a people of a loving and generous nature.

Hawaiian Ways

"In riding through Hawaiʻi," author Isabella Bird wrote, "I came everywhere upon traces of a once numerous population where the hill slopes are now only a wilderness of guava shrub, upon churches and schools all too large, while in some hamlets the voices of young children are altogether wanting." In some remote areas, the traditional grass-thatched houses, often modified with Western-style doors and windows, could still be found. Quietly and proudly, in about 1890, this family poses in their "Sunday best." [Baker–Van Dyke Collection]

Hawaiian Ways

An 'ohana, or Hawaiian family, poses in front of their abode for photographer Ray Jerome Baker. At the beginning of the twentieth century Baker traveled island-wide to photograph the vanishing lifestyle of the native people. [Baker–Van Dyke Collection]

The coconut tree provided the Hawaiians with material for many uses. Its leaves were excellent for weaving light and attractive hats. [Baker–Van Dyke Collection]

[Hawai'i State Archives]

Hawaiian woman weaving a mat from the cured leaves of the hala or pandanus tree. Hala provided a flexible, durable, and attractive material for handcrafting of many useful items. [Baker–Van Dyke Collection]

45

Hawaiian Ways

Many ancient Hawaiian customs still survive. This group has participated in a hukilau or hauling in of a long fishnet. The catch was shared by all, though in this case the results are meager. [Baker–Van Dyke Collection]

In this stylized photograph taken at the end of the nineteenth century, a Hawaiian fisherman prepares to cast his throw net. While traditional lifestyles and fishing practices continued long after U.S. annexation of the Islands, such posed photographs were intended to evoke a romantic mood of nostalgia for the "passing Polynesian race" for commercial or artistic purposes. [Hawai'i State Archives] or [Baker–Van Dyke Collection]

Hawaiian fishermen in 1936 wear the traditional malo or loincloth worn by Hawaiian men in the old days. [Hawai'i State Archives]

For Hawaiians, kalo, or taro, was the basis of life. Legends describe kalo as being the brother of the first human beings, buried and transformed into the nutritious plant. Whether planting, weeding, harvesting or cooking taro, it was the work of families. In this 1890 photograph taken in Hilo, several generations within an 'ohana clean, cook, and pound the kalo into a thick substance called poi. [Baker–Van Dyke Collection]

Pa'ū riders in Kapi'olani Park, June 11, 1900. The word pa'ū refers to the voluminous wraparound skirts worn by women riders both as a protection for their clothing like a cowboy's chaps and for decorative effect. The pa'ū was originally the tapa cloth garment worn by Hawaiian women in pre-Western-contact times. [Baker–Van Dyke Collection]

Ioane Haʻa, a paniolo from Pūʻuōʻō Ranch of Mauna Kea. Paniolo (Hawaiian cowboy) is a Hawaiian-language version of the word "Español." Hawaiʻi's first cowboys were Spanish-speaking cowboys brought in from Mexico for their skill at ranching tasks. Hawaiians took to cattle ranching with great enthusiasm. The name paniolo is still used today. [Hawaiʻi State Archives]

A kupuna, or elder, such as Kuluwaimaka, a former court chanter for King Kalākaua, was a "living treasure" of the ancient ways. His art was recorded during his presentations at the then Lalani Village in Waikīkī, which stood on the Lemon estate near Kapiʻolani Park. [Baker–Van Dyke Collection]

Hawaiian girls with ʻukuleles and guitars, 1908. [Baker–Van Dyke Collection]

Hula

Despite efforts of missionaries among the non-Hawaiian population, hula never became extinct. Although it faded from public sight during the middle decades of the nineteenth century, this authentic native dance form was still quietly and surreptitiously performed among the rural people.

When Westerners arrived in the islands, hula was Hawai'i's living theater, danced as an accompaniment to poetry. It could also be a religious rite to honor gods and chiefs. It was often dedicated to Laka, goddess of the hula. The ancient Hawaiian dances were performed by both men and women, though not usually at the same time. There were many sorts of hula: hula with gourds, drums, sticks, pebbles, hula with puppets, sacred hula, profane hula.

Mistakes in sacred hulas were believed to be bad omens, and were avoided at all costs. Dancers who wanted to learn these serious hulas took part in retreats given by master teachers, or kumu hulas, during which they put themselves under the protection of Laka.

The profane hula entertained and gladdened the hearts of both the ali'i class and the common people. Most of today's dances are descended from this popular type of hula.

Early missionaries disliked the hula they saw. The sight of scantily clad women offended them, thus they made great efforts to abolish the dance once their authority had been established.

Several of Hawai'i's monarchs recognized that the extinction of hula would mean the end of an important cultural tradition. They saw how their people had been demoralized by the destruction of other aspects of their civilization, thus they encouraged hula's revival despite missionary objections.

King David Kalākaua was particularly enthusiastic about reviving the hula in all its splendor and joy. He patronized kumu hulas and hula troupes. Accompanying photos show some of these troupes. One taken circa 1900 is remarkable for its time because the girls are shown with their breasts exposed, in the traditional manner of their forebears. For a time, the hulas of Hawai'i were in danger of disappearing forever. Thanks to the foresight and wisdom of Hawai'i's kings, Hawai'i's unique and graceful national dances are still seen today and are more popular than ever.

These grass-skirted young hula dancers of King Kalākaua's time, grouped around a large skin drum, bare their breasts for the photographer, and for the travelers who purchased such souvenirs. [Hawai'i State Archives]

49

Hula

King Kalākaua was delighted with the public demonstrations of ancient hula at his coronation on February 12, 1883, and his fiftieth birthday jubilee on November 16, 1886. Both occasions were attempts to revive his nation's pride. Native Hawaiian culture was to be praised and glorified, he believed, not hidden or denigrated as sinful or heathen. The dancers at the king's jubilee posed for their photograph standing before another treasure of native craftmanship—a display of Hawaiian quilts presented for his birthday. [Hawaiian Historical Society]

Ioane Ukeke, pictured with his hula dancers, was one of the famed chanters at King Kalākaua's court. He helped perpetuate and preserve the ancient oli, mele, and hula that had been handed down through the generations. [Hawai'i State Archives]

In this photo taken in the 1870s the girls wear long dresses covered by tapa cloth wraparound skirts. Despite suppression, the hula survived. Though many ancient hulas have been forgotten, the Hawaiian dance is currently evolving under the tutelage of present day Hawaiians. [Baker–Van Dyke Collection]

Toplessness was not the norm during the late nineteenth century. Many photographers staged these shots to appeal to the romanticized images of exotic beauty. [Baker–Van Dyke Collection]

The missionary-inspired criticism of the ancient oli, mele, and hula did not eliminate their performances before the reign of King Kalākaua, but certainly stifled teachers and performers. These early photographs of dancers in Honolulu and posed in a studio during the 1870s, demonstrate that hula had not died out before its revival by King Kalākaua. In many ways, these images of hula dancers and musicians at the end of the century reflected a native soul shaking off the shame of an imposed foreign morality and searching for life in the spirit of the ancient past. [Hawai'i State Archives]

Sweet Agriculture

Plantation towns were lonely isolated places in the midst of vast sugar cane fields far removed from other towns and cities. The homes of the workers were dominated by the mill structures. Shown here is Maui's Wailuku Sugar Mill in central Maui at the turn of the century. [Hawai'i State Archives]

Sweet Agriculture

Sugar cane was one of the food plants brought along to Hawai'i by the Polynesian settlers in their great canoe voyages from southern Polynesia. In the journal of his voyage to Hawai'i, Captain Cook mentioned seeing sugar cane in Hawaiian gardens.

There were sporadic attempts at commercial sugar cane growing and the manufacture of sugar in the early 1800s. Boki, the Governor of O'ahu, entered a partnership with English agriculturist John Wilkinson in 1825 and established a plantation in Honolulu's Mānoa Valley. The first long-lasting sugar plantation was begun by Ladd & Co. on Kaua'i in 1835.

Until the late 1840s and the early 1850s there was no imperative for expansion of the sugar industry, although the early missionaries recognized the need to expand and diversify Hawai'i's economy, which depended heavily on the visits of the huge whaling fleets. The California Gold Rush in 1849 provided a temporary stimulus, since Hawai'i's sugar found a ready market that paid high prices. But by 1851 the Gold Rush was over and the lucrative West Coast market collapsed. However, by the end of the 1850s, the West Coast market recovered as the populations of California and Oregon grew. As sugar prices went on the upswing, the number of sugar cane plantations began to grow.

The American Civil War proved to be a bonanza for the Hawaiian sugar industry as Southern sugar was no longer available. Prices for sugar zoomed so high that Hawaiian planters made a profit despite the high entry tariff paid at American ports. By 1866, Hawai'i was exporting almost eighteen million pounds of sugar, compared to a mere one-and-a-half million pounds only six years earlier. The real boon to the sugar industry was to come with the reciprocity treaty of 1876, which eliminated the heavy tariff on Hawaiian sugar entering U.S. ports.

As the sugar industry grew, it became apparent that a severe labor shortage was developing. Native Hawaiians were declining in numbers due to disease and a low birth rate, and had already contributed a high percentage of males to the plantation labor force. The solution was to import foreign contract labor in order to bolster the declining Island population and to combat the labor shortage. Where possible, Hawaiian authorities looked to recruit peoples with ethnic affinity to the Hawaiians, but the few Gilbert Islanders brought in from Micronesia were overcome by homesickness and proved most unsatisfactory. The majority of the laborers were to come from China, Japan, Korea, and the Philippines.

In the early days, life on the plantation was hard, and many contract workers left the plantations once their contracts expired. Under the contract labor system, refusal to work could be punished by imprisonment at hard labor until the offender consented to return. There were few provisions to protect the contract laborer from many forms of abuse. Whatever its drawbacks, the contract labor system brought new people to Hawai'i, people who eventually became American citizens and formed the backbone of Hawai'i's economy. Their descendants would become Hawai'i's future leaders.

The sugar industry constantly sought to improve its methods and the purity of its raw sugar, experimenting with new varieties of cane, new equipment, and techniques of growing, harvesting, and milling. Tunnels were dug through mountains; trestles and ditches were made to span valleys to carry water to irrigate dry but fertile lands. This allowed an enormous expansion of the acreage devoted to sugar cane. Former wastelands became green and productive, and Hawai'i gained a steady and dependable income from this vital agricultural industry.

Hawaiian Commercial & Sugar Company's mill at Pu'unēnē, Maui, was one of the first completely automated factories. [Hawai'i State Archives]

Sweet Agriculture

The exhausting labor required on sugar plantations was year-round, consisting of ten to twelve hours a day under the hot sun. Labor conditions were poor. By any measure, the contract labor system legitimatized by the Kingdom's Masters and Servants Act was indentured servitude. [Hawai'i State Archives]

A typical plantation house that dotted the cane fields. [Hawai'i State Archives]

The Spreckels mansion on Punahou Street photographed in 1908. Sumptuous and baronial, it was built at a cost of $100,000 in an age when the dollar was worth many times its present value. During the height of Spreckels's power, this Victorian palace was the scene of lavish dinner parties and dances. [Bishop Museum]

A San Francisco sugar refiner with an eye for opportunity, Spreckels cornered the 1877 Hawaiian sugar crop and rose to a position of power in the affairs of the Hawaiian Kingdom. As an advisor to King Kalākaua, he helped promote many dubious financial and political schemes. He purchased his power by bank rolling the free-spending king's pet projects at high rates of interest. In the end, Kalākaua found himself almost totally indebted to Spreckels. The shrewd Spreckels lost favor with the king through his displays of dictatorial behavior. Finally, he was bought off and left the Islands. A ruthless and unscrupulous businessman, he nevertheless contributed greatly to the expansion of the Hawaiian sugar industry. [Hawai'i State Archives]

Newcomers

The Hawaiians had been in the Islands for at least a thousand years when a new wave of people arrived, the first of several ethnic and national groups that would come to settle and eventually call Hawai'i their home. The first newcomers were people of European ancestry, beginning with the English under Captain Cook. Americans soon followed, coming as explorers, adventurers, businessmen, and missionaries.

At first, all foreigners were known as haole, or outsider. Since the first foreigners that the Hawaiians saw were Europeans, the word soon came to refer to persons of European ancestry. This interpretation continues to this day, and is sometimes used derogatorily.

For many decades after Hawai'i's initial contact with the outside world, the number of Caucasian residents in the Islands was very small. The early whites were missionaries, tradesmen, whaling and merchant seamen, and assorted others. Later, some whites were brought in as plantation laborers but, except for the Portuguese, they never formed a significant part of the plantation labor force.

Among the Caucasians who came in small groups as agricultural workers were Russians, Portuguese, Spaniards, Germans, and Norwegians. Since many of them, along with whites of American and British ancestry, intermarried with Hawaiians and other ethnic groups, it became difficult for census-takers to fit people into neat classifications as to who was Caucasian and who was not.

The 1853 census showed a white resident population of only 1,887. But throughout this early period, whites held influence and power far out of proportion to their numbers, a fact which led to considerable resentment. Many rose high in positions in government, as advisors to the Hawaiian monarchy. Others formed the core of the business establishment and held virtually uncontested economic power. Of course, not all Caucasians held great economic or political power. Many were people of modest means: professionals, tradesmen, and clerks. A few were paupers and derelicts, but certainly most were at least comfortably well-off compared to the Hawaiian population.

Newcomers of European ancestry were only the first in a series of population waves bringing in people from many countries who would eventually far outnumber the Native Hawaiian population. Next to come in large numbers were the Chinese, then the Japanese, Portuguese, Filipinos, Koreans, Puerto Ricans, and Samoans, as well as a liberal sprinkling of people from other parts of the world. Once here, they seldom kept exclusively to themselves, but mixed together in a potpourri of some of the most interesting ethnic mixtures to be found anywhere.

Hawai'i's multi-ethnic nature started with the arrival of Cook's expedition and continues to this day. The Hawaiians usually welcomed strangers, and the welcome could be warm indeed. The uninhibited and generous-natured Hawaiians set no ethnic barriers in choosing partners.

Within two generations of contact with the Western world, a mixed community had sprung up. Many of Hawai'i's oldest and most distinguished families are of such ancestry. At first, the combinations were predominantly Polynesian-European. Later, as the Chinese, Japanese, Filipinos, Portuguese, and many others arrived, the blendings became progressively more complicated and cosmopolitan.

Today, nearly fifty percent of all marriages in the state of Hawai'i are interracial. People of cosmopolitan ancestry, particularly part-Hawaiian, make up about one-fourth of the state's population. 2005 census analysis reveals that Hawai'i's resident population today can be broken down as follows: 25.3 percent Caucasian (compared to 18 percent in 1900), 16.5 percent Japanese, 22 percent Hawaiian or part-Hawaiian, 11.3 percent Filipino, 3.2 percent Chinese, 0.6 percent Korean, 0.8 percent Samoan/Tongan, and 2 percent African-American.

Newcomers

The Chinese

The first major group of indentured Chinese plantation workers arrived in 1852, although an individual Chinese was observed in 1794 in the retinue of King Kamehameha I at Kealakekua Bay, and it was rumored that a Chinese man living on Lānaʻi milled and boiled sugar in 1802.

Between 1852 and 1856, several thousand Chinese "coolies" were brought in to labor on the plantations. The census of 1878 counted a Chinese population of 6,045. By 1884, this number had risen to 18,254. The Chinese laborers were industrious and well-behaved, although they were quick to resent injustice. They were also intelligent and ambitious. As soon as their labor contracts were fulfilled, many headed straight for Honolulu and other towns to enter trade and open their own small businesses.

The Chinese who migrated to Hawaiʻi were mostly Cantonese from the Pearl River Delta near Macao. Another major dialect group among the immigrants were the Hakka who came from areas closer to Hong Kong. Because many Chinese dialects are mutually unintelligible, communication between the two groups of Chinese was often difficult. An observer in the year 1856 was amused to see two groups of Chinese who spoke differing dialects communicating with each other quite adequately by using the Hawaiian language, which they had learned while working on the plantations.

The Chinese laborers soon came to be considered a problem in Hawaiʻi because of their growing numbers and that they were mostly male. Quite a few married Hawaiian women, resulting in Hawaiian-Chinese families being common in Hawaiʻi today. Another reason for resentment was that the Chinese were astute and hardworking businessmen, offering competition to the other tradesmen. Before the end of the nineteenth century there were many rich Chinese families in Honolulu. The growing Chinese population, which so worried Hawaiʻi in the late 1880s, was soon to be outnumbered by the coming wave of Japanese.

By the 1870s the expanding sugar plantations faced labor shortages. Thousands of Chinese immigrants were lured to Hawaiʻi to work under three- or five-year contracts after which many moved into Honolulu's Chinatown, or took up independent rice and coffee farming. By the 1890s, Chinese were no longer considered "reliable" plantation laborers, and their immigration was limited to five thousand a year for agricultural labor only. [Hawaiʻi State Archives]

Hawai'i saw its first Japanese contract workers in 1868 when a small group of 148 were recruited, against the wishes of the Japanese government. It was not until 1886, when an agreement was signed between the governments of Hawai'i and Japan, that Japanese immigrants began to arrive in large numbers.

In 1890, the census listed 12,610 Japanese. The figure grew to 61,111 by 1900. Unlike the other countries from which contract workers originated, Japan carefully monitored how her citizens were being treated and regularly sent inspection teams to the plantations to take note of grievances. Japan also set up offices in Honolulu to facilitate the recruiting process and to oversee the welfare of those recruited.

By the early 1900s, Japanese made up some forty percent of Hawai'i's population. As the male laborers sent for their wives and children as well as mail-order brides, the Japanese population grew and hostility toward them mounted. One outgrowth of this hostility was the passage of the Federal Exclusion Act in 1924, which almost completely halted immigration from Japan.

Newly arrived Japanese agricultural workers with plantation housing in background. [Hawai'i State Archives]

The "picture bride" system was initiated to locate suitable mates for thousands of single men. These women traveled to Hawai'i to begin a marriage with a man they had, in most cases, never seen except in a photograph. After a quick ceremony, they were expected to perform the domestic duties of a wife, and also work on the plantation. [Hawai'i State Archives]

After the long, tedious passage from Japan, immigrant contract laborers would disembark at the port of Honolulu with all their worldly possessions bundled into their small baskets. [Hawai'i State Archives]

Newcomers

The Japanese

This photo shows, in microcosm, the assimilation of Hawai'i's immigrant groups. Originally recruited as contract labor for the sugar and pineapple plantations, one group after another—the Chinese, the Portuguese, the Japanese, the Filipinos—followed almost the same steps toward entry into the mainstream of Island life and Americanization. Once their plantation contracts were fulfilled, the oldest generation became small shop owners and tradesmen, leading self-sacrificing lives on meager incomes to ensure that their children would do better. The second generation, with advantages of education unavailable to their parents, entered professional and white-collar jobs. The gradually evolving lifestyles accompanying this change are reflected in the clothing worn when this photo was taken in 1928. It ranges from the somber, conservative garb of the older men and the old-country kimonos of the women to the American school-day dress of the children. Any doubt about the importance of Americans of Japanese ancestry was dispelled with the election of George Ariyoshi as governor of Hawai'i in 1974. His election did not depend solely on the Japanese-American vote: many Japanese voted for his opponents, and many non-Japanese voted for Ariyoshi. [Bishop Museum]

The majority of plantation laborers recruited to Hawai'i came from the Far East. However, some also emigrated from Europe. Of these, Portuguese from the Atlantic islands of Madeira and the Azores formed the largest contingent.

Most of the 17,500 Portuguese contract workers recruited for Hawai'i's plantations arrived between 1878 and 1887. The Hawaiian census counted 486 Portuguese in the Islands in 1878. By 1884, that number had risen to 9,967.

Like other plantation workers before them, the Portuguese were eager to leave the plantations once their contracts had expired. Some planters were unhappy with the Portuguese, who demanded higher salaries than Asians, were less submissive, and had recourse to the Portuguese Consulate. Though many Portuguese women and children accompanied their men to Hawai'i, intermarriage with Hawaiians was not uncommon. Today there are many persons of mixed Portuguese-Hawaiian ancestry.

Some Portuguese plantation workers who left work on sugar plantations set themselves up in business or bought plots of land for truck gardening.

This tiny Portuguese-owned store beside a remote country road sold staple supplies to plantation workers from nearby camps. [Multi-Cultural Center]

Portuguese women baking bread, 1908. The Portuguese clung to many of their national customs here in the Islands. These Portuguese women are baking pao doce or sweet bread in a backyard oven. Used communally, these ovens allowed one woman to bake enough bread on a single day to supply her family for a week. [Hawai'i State Archives]

Newcomers

The Portuguese

Above: Portuguese women plantation workers from the Atlantic islands of Madeira and the Azores wearing the picturesque hats of their distant homeland. Many Portuguese customs have survived in the new Hawaiian homeland, particularly as concerns food. Today, everyone in the Islands enjoys malasadas, a kind of fluffy doughnut without a hole, served hot and sprinkled with sugar. Portuguese bean soup is another highly appreciated item on Island restaurant menus.
[Bishop Museum]

Right: A Portuguese family get-together in Lahaina, Maui, about 1915. The Portuguese originally tended to settle together in local communities. One located on the slopes of Honolulu's Punchbowl Crater, is still a predominantly Portuguese area. Many others remain throughout the Islands.
[Hawai'i State Archives]

Newcomers

The Koreans

A few small groups of Korean merchants were present in Hawai'i as early as 1899, but it was not until January 13, 1903, that the first major group of immigrants arrived. This was marked by the arrival of the SS *Gaelic* from Inchon, Korea, which carried 101 persons—55 men, 21 women, and 25 children.

At this time plantation owners in Hawai'i were looking at Korea as a possible source of plantation labor. During the next two and a half years, sixty-five boatloads with 7,843 Korean laborers landed in Honolulu. Upon their arrival, the immigrants were scattered to plantations on O'ahu and the Big Island.

In April 1905, the emperor of Korea decreed the stoppage of emigration from his country because of official Korean concern over rumored distresses suffered by Koreans who had immigrated to Mexico. This threw a cloud of suspicion over all labor emigration.

Between 1911 and 1924, many of the bachelor Korean immigrants sent home for picture brides. Eight hundred Korean women arrived. Subsequently, the number of families increased and helped to stabilize the Korean population in Hawai'i.

Most of the Koreans had no desire to remain on plantations. Some started boarding houses: couples took in single Korean men as roomers and the women cooked. Other Koreans turned successfully to food manufacturing, tailoring, carpentry, laundry, and other trades.

A Korean family dressed up for a visit to the photographer's studio. The husband wears American clothing, but the more tradition-minded wife clings to her native Korean style of dress. [Hawai'i State Archives]

Newcomers

The Filipinos

The Filipinos were the last large-scale wave of immigrants recruited to Hawai'i as plantation laborers. They were drawn mainly from various agricultural populations within the Philippine Islands and were composed largely of single men. They left their villages, and families for the uncertainty of life on Hawai'i's sugar plantations. Of the approximately seventy-five thousand Filipino immigrants who came to Hawai'i between 1920 and 1929, sixty-five thousand, or eighty-five percent, were men who lived in separate Filipino camps. Having left their families, they treated each other as family. The men addressed each other with the respectful terms manong, or older male, tata, or elder brother, and bayaw, or brother-in-law, even if they had no blood or marriage relationship. As children were born within the community to the few Filipino couples, it was customary at baptisms to have a hundred kumpadre, or sponsors, chosen so that the older ties of the family were extended to a larger circle of the immigrants. These familial bonds were essential to ease the hardships of immigrant life and to enrich their social world with love and friendship.

As the last immigrant group to Hawai'i in large numbers, Filipinos have just started to have full opportunity to move up the social and economic ladder. Politically, their power became apparent with the election of a Filipino governor, Ben Cayetano.

A Filipino worker's family awaits the father's return from his labors at the door of their tiny plantation-town house. [Hawai'i State Archives]

Newcomers

The Puerto Ricans

Much is made of Hawai'i's rainbow mixture of peoples resulting from the intermarriage of people of diverse ethnic backgrounds. However, the Puerto Ricans arrived in Hawai'i already ethnically mixed. The basic ancestry of the Puerto Rican people consists of pre-Columbian Indians, Caucasians of Spanish origin, and blacks of African descent. After centuries of intermingling, Puerto Rican families carried genes of all three groups in varying amounts.

On December 23, 1900, the ship *Rio de Janeiro* entered Honolulu Harbor with the first large group of Puerto Ricans brought to Hawai'i for plantation work. In the years 1900 and 1901, some 5,200 more came to try their fortunes in Hawai'i, prompted by severe hurricane destruction in their home island. About 2,400 were men who had signed a three-year agricultural contract; the remainder were women and children.

Due to some similarities in culture and general appearance, the Puerto Ricans intermarried frequently with Filipinos, Portuguese, Spaniards, and Hawaiians. Puerto Rican families grew rapidly since they were among the few immigrant groups that initially included women and children. The 1950 census, the last in Hawai'i that counted Puerto Ricans as a separate group, counted a Puerto Rican population of ten thousand.

To a great extent the Puerto Ricans have melded into the general population of Hawai'i, not really considering themselves a separate group. Nevertheless, many of the older people still speak Spanish and prepare their delicious food specialties, a cuisine similar to traditional Cuban fare. In line with recent trends among various ethnic groups, Hawaiians of Puerto Rican ancestry are showing a renewed interest in their cultural and ancestral background.

Mary and Basilio Salcedo, brother and sister, born in Hawai'i to parents who emigrated from Puerto Rico. This portrait was taken in 1915. [Hawai'i State Archives]

Newcomers

The Samoans

The majority of the diverse peoples who came to Hawai'i were originally brought in as plantation labor and later moved out of the plantations to join Hawai'i's mainstream. Few of these peoples, however, were Polynesians and ethnically and culturally akin to the Native Hawaiians. Gilbertese and a few other Pacific Islanders were recruited for plantation work, but they were small in number and totally unsuited to the hard and monotonous labor. Eventually most of them returned to their home islands and there was no further recruitment of Pacific Islanders.

The Samoan migration to Hawai'i was unique because the Samoans did not come as plantation workers, and they were the first significant group of Polynesian migrants to Hawai'i. Samoa consists of a group of islands about three thousand miles slightly southwest of Hawai'i. It is now believed that in the islands of Samoa and nearby Tonga, the Polynesians first became a ethnically and culturally distinct people, later voyaging forth to discover the vast skein of islands that today comprise what is known as Polynesia.

The first large group of Samoans came to Hawai'i in 1919 when the Mormon, or LDS temple was built in Lā'ie on O'ahu's northeastern shore. The Mormon Church had long taken root in Samoa. At Lā'ie they formed a primarily agricultural group, which by 1950 numbered about five hundred people.

In 1952 about one thousand Samoans arrived in Hawai'i. They were mostly naval personnel and their dependents transferred here due to the phasing out of the U.S. naval base on Tutuila, the main island of American Samoa. As American nationals, the Samoans were able to enter Hawai'i without going through immigration procedures. It is estimated that there are presently more than thirteen thousand Samoans and part-Samoans residing in Hawai'i, the majority of them on O'ahu.

To a great extent, Hawai'i's Samoans have preserved their colorful ways, and the Samoan language is in daily use in Samoan communities. The Samoans come from an area of Polynesia where the ancient traditions are still surprisingly intact despite centuries of contact with the Western world. Strongly patriotic, with love and pride for their homeland and its culture, Samoans here and at home have long practiced "Fa'a Samoa" which means "the Samoan Way." The immigrants have taught their children pride in the culture and language of Samoa. This has helped preserve the old Samoan way of life.

Samoan culture has traditionally exalted cooperation and submission to chiefs and elders as opposed to individualism. To some extent, this lack of competitive spirit has been a hindrance to progress in today's Western culture. While the chieftainship structure is still strong, it is meeting increasing resistance from youngsters more exposed than their parents to Western ways. Samoan communal ideas of property have also caused conflict in a society where property is considered an individual rather than a group possession.

One of O'ahu's most colorful events is held every year when the Samoan community celebrates Flag Day in memory of the time when American Samoa came under the American flag. It is on this day that all the bright colors are worn, traditional dances are danced, and soaring a cappella songs are sung amidst huge quantities of Samoan foods spread out for one and all. It is a day when Samoans from all walks of life lay aside their Western clothes and put on lava-lavas and face paint to relive the ancient times.

Samoan girls share something funny. Sometimes younger Samoans face a confilct of values between the old ways and life in Hawai'i. [Baker–Van Dyke Collection]

Other Pacific Islander groups that have settled in Hawai'i include Tongans and Micronesians. The Tongans, who now number four thousand, originally began coming in 1965 under the auspices of the Mormon Church. Micronesians from Palau, Guam, the Marquesas, and the Marshall Islands began arriving in significant numbers in 1986 and now have a population of eight thousand.

Honolulu

Honolulu grew up beside a harbor that once boasted only a tiny village of grass-thatched houses on a dusty plain. The name of this village was Kou. By 1857, Honolulu, which means "protected harbor," had become one of the Pacific's major seaports, prospering on the whaling fleets and merchantmen plying between the West Coast and Asia.

Honolulu was the best port in the Islands. It offered the safest anchorage, the only shipyard, and the biggest town.

Consequently, it soon sheltered the greatest number of ships. The resulting prosperity was reflected in the improved façade of downtown Honolulu. There were mean and sordid streets in 1857, but over time the general demeanor and appearance of the city's business center rapidly improved. As wealth brought pride, Honolulu's affluent merchants and business establishments began to impose an orderliness and solidity previously unknown.

This early 1860s view of downtown Honolulu looks mauka, or toward the mountains, to Nu'uanu Valley. Photographer Henry L. Chase's studio at Fort and Hotel streets in the left foreground is identified by its sign, Hale Pa'iki'i (House of Photography). He and others, such as J. J. Williams and A. A. Montano, made portraits of people from all walks of life, and documented the rapidly changing face of the city's streets. [Hawai'i State Archives]

65

King Kalākaua's reputation for enjoying soirées, dances, drinking, horse racing, lavish parties, and gambling—although often exaggerated by his enemies—was not without basis. Kalākaua entertained friends and visitors of the Royal Boat House at Honolulu Harbor far from the watchful eyes of the missionary community. [Hawai'i State Archives]

An 1884 view of Nu'uanu Avenue taken from the harbor. [Hawai'i State Archives]

Kawaiahaʻo Church, designed by Rev. Hiram Bingham, was built by Hawaiian labor with coral blocks cut from the reefs of Honolulu. Weighing over a ton each, over fourteen thousand blocks were cut underwater, lifted from the reef, hauled to the construction site, and then hoisted into place with Herculean effort. The church was used not only for worship, but also for important commemorations. [Hawaiʻi State Archives]

This 1856 view of King Street looking toward Waikīkī was taken from the corner of Fort Street in downtown Honolulu. The area just beyond was largely residential, occupied by such prominent citizens as Princess Bernice Pauahi and Charles Reed Bishop, whose two-story house with its spacious lanai, or veranda, is visible on the left. In later years the Bishop home was converted into the Arlington Hotel, the site of "Camp Boston," the 1893 headquarters for U.S. military troops during the overthrow of the monarchy. Kawaiahaʻo Church, with its original wooden steeple, is in the distance. [H. Stangenwald / Bishop Museum]

Honolulu

The heart of Honolulu's shopping district was Fort Street, photographed here near the corner of Hotel Street circa 1895. In 1903, the mule- and horse-drawn trolleys of Hawaiian Tramways Ltd. were replaced with the electric cars of the Honolulu Rapid Transit & Land Co. [Hawai'i State Archives]

Chinatown residents flee with their belongings. [Bishop Museum]

The fire's devastation was staggering; thirty acres of the city became charred rubble. [Hawai'i State Archives]

Bordered by River Street, Beretania, Nu'uanu, and the waterfront, Hawai'i's Chinatown is the oldest in the United States, inhabited mostly by Hawaiians and Asian immigrants. Its dense population lived and worked in streets crowded with wooden stores, tenements, and highly flammable warehouses.

On April 18, 1886, it was destroyed by flames when a fire broke out at a restaurant on the corner of Smith and Hotel streets. Three days later, the raging fire had burned the homes of 7,000 Chinese and 350 Hawaiians, leaving eight blocks of the district a smoldering heap of charred remains, though the twin spires of Kaumakapili Church were unharmed by the blaze.

Although strict fire codes were enacted by the legislature after the conflagration, the rebuilding of Chinatown went so fast that little attention was paid to the regulations. Fourteen years later, Chinatown burned to the ground again when an inferno wiped out a large section of Hawai'i's capital city.

An outbreak of bubonic plague during the last weeks of 1899 led city authorities to take quick action. To control the spread of the bubonic plague, the Honolulu Fire Department in December 1899 began to burn down the Chinatown buildings where victims of the dreaded disease had been found. The entire district was quarantined. Thousands of residents were given antiseptic baths and had their clothing burned. Under the watchful eye of the health department, they were taken in drays to quarantine areas.

On the morning of January 20, 1900, fires were set to burn out plague-infested houses near Beretania Street and Nu'uanu Avenue. High winds suddenly began to gust and the flames leaped to the Waikīkī spire of Kaumakapili Church. As the fire department worked frantically to control the flames, the other spire exploded into a fiery inferno. Flames leaped over Beretania Street and raced uncontrolled toward the harbor. Panic-stricken residents fled down King Street as Citizens Guard members used ax handles, baseball bats, and pickets torn hastily from fences to keep the crowds from leaving the quarantined sections of town.

When the fire had finally burned itself out, the devastation was staggering. Thirty acres of the city, looking mauka toward Beretania Street, were nothing but charred rubble. Kaumakapili Church was left a burned-out shell. Thousands of Chinese, Japanese, and Hawaiian residents of the populated district were left homeless, most of their belongings destroyed in the conflagration. Though many of the victims bitterly suspected that the fire had been started deliberately by the haole authorities to destroy the Asian section of town, the process of rebuilding Chinatown with more fire-resistant materials soon began.

Honolulu

Royal Hawaiian Band

Captain Henry Berger, founder and leader for many years, stands in front of the Royal Hawaiian Band, which was formed in 1836. Berger helped to reorganize the Royal Hawaiian Band in 1872 and assumed full leadership in 1877. For over thirty-five years he led the musicians in numerous performances until his retirement in 1915. No major event in old Honolulu was complete without a band performance. The famed band has played all over the world and has survived through the overthrow of the monarchy, annexation, and statehood. To this day, the Royal Hawaiian Band performs every Friday in the bandstand on the grounds of the ʻIolani Palace. [Hawaiʻi State Archives]

One of the favorite pastimes of visitors to Honolulu in the 1880s was taking a leisurely carriage to the summit of Pūowaina, or the "Hill of Sacrifice." From the slopes of this ancient volcanic crater known also as Punchbowl, there were stunning views of the town, the 'Ewa plains, and the districts of Makiki, Mō'ili'ili, Waikīkī, and Diamond Head. On the slopes of the crater was a battery of small cannon used to salute arriving and departing ships, to honor special events, and to mourn the passing of kings. By 1900 a sixteen-foot-wide road had been macadamized to allow the first motorized traffic to maneuver the steep and winding windswept path. [Hawai'i State Archives]

Elderly Hawaiian men like these in the photograph sold lauhala fans, mats, and hats on the streets of Honolulu, particularly on "Boat Days." Other notable vendors were the manapua men selling delectable Chinese treats. These street merchants added a colorful touch to the town. [Baker–Van Dyke Collection]

The Hawaiian outrigger canoe with Diamond Head in the background was a favorite subject in the first photographs used to attract visitors to the Islands. The canoes were made from hollowed-out logs of koa wood. [Baker–Van Dyke Collection]

This peaceful beach scene, looking toward Diamond Head, was taken long before Waikīkī became a mecca for Hawai'i's visitors. In simpler days it was a quiet strip of coconut palm-lined beach. Hawaiian royalty and well-to-do citizens kept beach cottages in Waikīkī as hideaways from the cares of everyday life. [Hawai'i State Archives]

In 1902, a trip to Waikīkī was a happy outing in this quaint trolley. The picture was taken at the juncture of McCully and Kalākaua. This area was still devoted to banana, rice, and taro patches. The Moana Hotel is barely visible in the distance below the crest of Diamond Head. In 1903, the mule-drawn cars of the Hawaiian Tramways Company were replaced by the electric trolleys of the Honolulu Rapid Transit Company. Now both visitors and residents could go in greater comfort to the popular bathing beaches at Waikīkī. [Baker–Van Dyke Collection]

Surfing and canoe paddling, the water sports of ancient Hawai'i, fascinated early visitors to Waikīkī. Circa 1910–1915 [Hawaiian Historical Society]

With the rapid urban growth of Honolulu came the blight of industrialization as the harbor area was filled in to expand much-needed commercial services such as those provided by the Honolulu Iron Works. Since the 1850s, the Honolulu Iron Works had provided the Islands with the building materials essential for the successful construction of sugar mills, commercial structures, and residential housing. Eventually the residential districts near the harbor, including Iwilei and Kaka'ako, would also become industrial areas with acres of unattractive warehouses, fuel tanks, and supply yards. [Bishop Museum]

The U.S. annexation of the Hawaiian Islands in 1898 had been justified by its supporters as a necessary strategy for the protection of American interests in the Pacific against the growing presence of Japan. By establishing a naval base at Pearl Harbor, these strategists urged, the United States would have a powerful dominion over the future of the Pacific region. The construction of a dry dock at Pearl Harbor was essential to the long-range plan of making Hawai'i the center of operations for the U.S. Navy's Pacific Fleet. On August 21, 1919, the dry dock was finally opened with an elaborate ceremony. "Pearl Harbor," wrote a prophetic editor of one of the Honolulu newspapers a few years earlier, "is going to settle the destiny of the world." [Library of Congress]

TWENTIETH CENTURY: 1900–1950

The first of the first-class hotels in Hawai'i was the brainchild of Dr. John Mott-Smith, a Honolulu dentist. With the strong support of Kamehameha V, he was able to raise both government and private funds to complete the luxurious, graceful hotel at a final cost of over $116,000. The Hawaiian Hotel, as it was originally called, opened on February 29, 1872, with a luxurious subscription ball. When the travel writer Isabella Bird visited the hotel one year later, she referred to it as "the perfection of a hotel." [Library of Congress]

The Military

After annexation, the United States military moved swiftly to transform the Islands into a Western defense perimeter for the expanding U.S. presence in Asia. Parades and reviews were frequent, as seen in this photo of cavalry marching in downtown Honolulu. [Hawai'i State Archives]

Right: Established in 1909, the 14,400 acres of Schofield Barracks constitute the largest American military base in the United States. Schofield Barracks is located in the center of the island of O'ahu. It was home to the Hawaiian Division of the United States Army, which during the 1930s had been reinforced to a strength of over twenty thousand soldiers. In addition to Schofield Barracks, the Hawaiian Division consisted of airbases at Wahiawā's Wheeler Field and Luke Field on Ford Island at Pearl Harbor, and a coastal and harbor defense system at Fort DeRussy, Fort Ruger, and Fort Armstrong. U.S. troops were stationed at the entrance to Pearl Harbor at Fort Kamehameha, and the entire operations of the Hawaiian Department were headquartered at Fort Shafter. With the U.S. Army's Hawaiian Division under General Walter C. Short and the Pacific Fleet of the United States Navy at Pearl Harbor under Admiral Husband E. Kimmel, the military believed, in 1941, that America's might in the Pacific was invincible. [National Archives]

From a military perspective, Hawai'i's strategic location had long made the Islands a desirable acquisition for the United States. Ships of the U.S. Navy regularly called throughout the nineteenth century, and the navy saw Pearl Harbor as a potential base. Annexation became more urgent when it was suddenly recognized that Hawai'i was an important halfway point for refreshing troops headed to the Philippines during the Spanish-American War and the ensuing nationalist insurrections. Negotiations proceeded at full speed and American soldiers were already on their way from California, arriving just four days after the official annexation date of August 12, 1898.

The Army. The first U.S. Army encampment was set up at a site in Kapi'olani Park when infantry and engineer elements paused here en route to the Philippines. Called Camp McKinley, it was the only military establishment in the territory until 1907, when Fort Shafter was built.

With annexation, the army was faced with the task of defending the new territory. In 1908, work was begun on a new major military post on the Leilehua plateau of central O'ahu. This post was named Schofield Barracks to honor Civil War Lt. Gen. John M. Schofield, who had earlier visited Hawai'i and recommended the acquisition of Pearl Harbor for the navy. Wheeler Field, at the south end of Schofield, was established by the Army Air Corps in 1922. Construction of Hickam Field began in 1935. Later, the Army Air Corps became a separate branch of service, the air force.

The Navy. The first U.S. Navy ship to visit Hawai'i anchored in Honolulu Harbor in 1826. Some twenty-five years before annexation, the navy built a coaling station in Honolulu. Construction of the giant Pearl Harbor naval complex began in 1909 and the USS *California* became the first U.S. warship to enter Pearl Harbor in 1911.

The Marines. The marine corps first moved into Pearl Harbor barracks in 1923.

In 1953 the former Naval Air Station at Kāne'ohe was recommissioned as a Marine Corps Air Station.

The Coast Guard. Coast guard cutters have been patrolling Hawaiian waters since the Spanish-American War. Today the Hawai'i-based coast guard supervises a vast area of the central Pacific, ranging as far as Alaska and Samoa.

World War I. Hawai'i and the military forces stationed here played a minor part in the affairs of World War I. Nine German naval vessels were seized upon the outbreak of hostilities between Germany and the U.S. The vessels had previously sought sanctuary here from the Japanese Navy in 1914 during America's period of neutrality.

World War II and Afterwards. By the late 1930s it became obvious that the U.S. and Japan would clash in the Pacific, and the military establishment in Hawai'i grew larger each year. After the December 7, 1941, Pearl Harbor surprise attack, martial law was declared. Hawai'i remained under military rule until October 19, 1944. Life for Island residents under martial law was difficult: most normal civil rights were suspended, and curfews and restrictions were imposed. The press was heavily censored, especially the two Japanese-American dailies that were allowed to continue printing. Wages of all workers were frozen and work absenteeism was punishable by jail sentence. Some have argued that there was no real need for such a lengthy period of military control.

During the Korean and Vietnam conflicts, the Islands served as a staging area as well as a popular rest and recuperation center. Today, defense is a major industry in Hawai'i. With the U.S. withdrawing from key Asian bases and the Asian Theater remaining a risk area, Hawai'i is as important as ever as a military base.

It quickly became the custom during World War II for arriving ships, particularly these carrying troops, to be greeted by hula dancers. [Bob Ebert Collection]

The Big Five

Bishop Street in downtown Honolulu became the financial center of the Hawaiian Islands as most of the "Big Five" companies and financial institutions, including the Bishop Bank and Bank of Hawai'i, located along its wide, palm tree–lined sidewalks. The Dillingham Transportation Building is photographed in 1929 at its location at the corner of Queen and Bishop streets. The Dillingham name was synonymous with railroads in Hawai'i; the company and its Oahu Railway and Land Co. trains controlled all railroad transportation on O'ahu. [Hawai'i State Archives]

Two blocks mauka on Bishop Street, the first-class Alexander Young Hotel opened in 1903; it was built at a cost of $2,000,000. The imposing 465-foot Colusa sandstone facade extended along the Waikīkī side of Bishop Street from King to Hotel Street. [Hawai'i State Archives]

A few blocks away, at the corner of Chaplain Lane and Fort Street, was the more modest Blaisdell Hotel whose marble-floored lobby was among the first in the Islands. [Baker–Van Dyke Collection]

While many Honolulu buildings were constructed to reflect American tastes, the architects C. W. Dickey and Hart Wood developed a distinctive "Hawaiian architecture" suitable to the community's Polynesian and Asian character and tropical climate. Envisioning a unique urban setting which reflected Island themes, they designed such masterpieces as the Alexander & Baldwin Building built in 1930 on Bishop Street. Its high-pitched roof, Mediterranean stucco façade, Asian motifs and palm-tree landscaping were features of "Hawaiian architecture." [Hawai'i State Archives]

A Strange Reunion

If Sanford B. Dole (left), former president of the short-lived Republic of Hawai'i, and Lili'uokalani, former queen of the Kingdom of Hawai'i, seem less than pleased on the occasion of this photograph; they have good reason. Dole was instrumental in the forceful overthrow, which brought an end to the Hawaiian monarchy and later subjected the queen to the humiliation of house arrest in an apartment in her own 'Iolani Palace. Each felt that he or she was perfectly justified in his or her actions. Perhaps in the twenty years that had passed before this gathering was recorded they resumed their original friendship. If they had, it certainly does not show in the grim looks on their faces. This meeting was arranged by Henry Berger (standing), leader of the Royal Hawaiian Band for forty years. Berger brought the two together in the interests of patriotic solidarity and to elicit public support of American aid to the Allied cause in World War I. While neither Dole nor the former queen was overjoyed at the idea of meeting, each may have felt that their public meeting would evoke good feelings on the part of all Hawaiian citizens. The nervously uncomfortable observer on the right was the governor of the Territory of Hawai'i, Lucius E. Pinkham. [Hawai'i State Archives]

Early Waikīkī was a charming place of rolling surf, cool breezes, lush taro farms, and abundant fish ponds. During the nineteenth and early twentieth centuries, both Hawaiian royalty and the sugar industry elite retreated to its relaxing shores. When tourism burst upon the scene in the first three decades of the twentieth century, Waikīkī was the natural location for the development of new hotels such as the Moana, the Seaside, the Waikīkī Tavern, and the elegant Royal Hawaiian Hotel. The construction of the Ala Wai Canal in the 1920s allowed the wetlands of Waikīkī to be drained, paving the way for development. In this image, a trolley moves along Kalākaua Avenue just in front of the Cleghorn beach house. Already, the bungalow-style houses that would characterize Waikīkī's neighborhoods had begun to proliferate on the mauka, or mountain, side of the street. These quaint cottages would eventually disappear, casualties of the high-rise construction frenzy that would sweep through Waikīkī in the sixties and seventies. Circa 1927–1930. [Hawai'i State Archives]

Duke Kahanamoku: Surfing

No person was more synonymous with Hawai'i in the first half of the twentieth century than Duke Kahanamoku, the famed surfer, swimmer, Olympic gold medalist, small businessman, sheriff of Honolulu, and unofficial ambassador of the Islands. Born in 1890, Kahanamoku was raised in Waikīkī, where he attended grammar school and spent all his free time in the ocean. Leaving school as a teenager, he spent his days with other beachboys, helping to form Hui Nalu or "Club of the Waves." At the age of twenty-one, he was discovered swimming like a fish at Sans Souci beach by William T. Rawlins, a lawyer and water sports enthusiast who became Duke's first coach. Rawlins helped organize the first Hawaiian Amateur Athletic Union swimming competitions at Honolulu Harbor on August 11, 1911. On that memorable day, six-foot-one-inch tall Kahanamoku broke the world's record in the hundred-yard freestyle by 4.6 seconds. Amazingly, that same day he broke the world's record for the fifty-yard freestyle swim. At the 1912 Olympic Games held at Stockholm, Sweden, the "human fish" from Hawai'i won the gold medal in the hundred-meter freestyle competitions, a feat he repeated at the Antwerp games in 1920.

The worldwide fame which Kahanamoku earned at the Olympic Games was extended to his Island home. Photographs of Duke surfing at Waikīkī were published in tourism brochures and advertisements promoting Waikīkī.

Wherever he went, Duke demonstrated the Hawaiian sport of surfing to fascinated crowds. In Australia, California, and on the Atlantic Coast, he won thousands of converts who began building their own boards and experimenting with new techniques of surfing and board construction.

A mild-mannered, quiet-spoken Hawaiian gentleman who always expressed humility in reference to his own fame, Duke's later career included acting in Hollywood films. In 1932, he was elected the sheriff of Honolulu, an office to which he won re-election for many years. When Duke died suddenly of a heart attack in January 1968, Hawai'i had lost its favorite Hawaiian son. In a tradition befitting royalty, his ashes were taken out to sea amongst a flotilla of canoes and scattered in the waters of his beloved Waikīkī.

After a temporary decline during World War II, surfing became popular again in the 1950s. Light balsa-wood boards soon replaced the heavy and clumsy redwood boards that had previously been common. Innovators were constantly improving board designs, seeking lightness and maneuverability. Today's surfboards are fairly standardized in design and size, ranging between six and eight feet in length. Hawai'i is now the scene for many worldwide surfing competitions, which are most often held during the winter in the mountainous surf of the North Shore and Mākaha areas of O'ahu. Every year, surfing greats from everywhere in the world gather to compete. [Hawai'i State Archives]

Surfing

Hawaiian swimmers who were members of the 1920 U.S. Olympic swim team. Back row (from left): Warren Kealoha, Ludy Langer, Duke Kahanamoku, and George "Dad" Center. Front row: "Wild Wild Bill" Harris, Helen "Moses" Cassidy, and Pua Kealoha. Not in the photo: Harold "Stubby" Kruger, Kahili Boyd, Joe Gilman, Fred Kahele, and George Kane. [Hawai'i State Archives]

In addition to its beaches, gentle swelling surf and graceful trade winds Waikīkī also offered its visitors the opportunity to meet its famed "beachboys." In this photo, taken in front of the old Moana hotel pier, they are headed by Duke Kahanamoku. Circa 1920. [Baker–Van Dyke Collection]

Boat Days

Lei sellers vend their colorful creations on a downtown sidewalk in the early 1900s. Business was especially brisk on Steamer Day as residents rushed to buy greeting leis for newly arrived visitors. "My first impression," wrote poet and man-about-town Don Blanding of his arrival at Honolulu on "Steamer Day, was that the town had attended a masquerade party that night before and had remained in motley to greet the steamer…" [Hawai'i State Archives]

Boat Days

The arrival of any large ship at Honolulu Harbor was always a cause of joy and expectation. One never knew what the ship might bring—mail, unexpected friends, a long-awaited cargo. It soon became a tradition to greet ships as they pulled into the dock, particularly when the advent of steam power inaugurated an era of dependable scheduled service.

Before long, the greeting began to take on a more ceremonial aspect. The Royal Hawaiian Band enlivened the events with stirring martial airs and sentimental tunes of greeting and farewell. Word was passed as soon as the lookout on Diamond Head spotted an arriving steamer. Fleets of yachts and boats went out to escort the steamer into the harbor, and there would later be on-boat parties for passengers, crews, and greeters.

Among the many picturesque dockside sights on Steamer Day were the lines of Hawaiian lei sellers stringing flowers of a hundred varieties in every possible combination and vending their floral wares to greeters and the newly arrived and soon departing. On departing streamers, there grew a tradition of throwing one's lei overboard as the ship left the harbor. If the leis drifted back to shore (as they usually did) it meant that one would return.

Steamer Day, Honolulu.

The steamer has arrived and the dockside street is alive with hurrying greeters and floral lei vendors. Circa 1915. [Bob Ebert]

Labor Turmoil

The Honolulu Advertiser
Hawaii's Territorial Newspaper

HONOLULU, TERRITORY OF HAWAII, WEDNESDAY MORNING, SEPTEMBER 10, 1924.

PRICE FIVE CENTS.

17 DEAD, MANY INJURED AS POLICE, STRIKERS CLASH

CHANG MOVES BIG ARMY TO SHANHAIKWAN

Sonoma Gets S.O.S. From Steamer Piled on Reef

Kauai Scene Of Wholesale Slaying When Filipinos At Hanapepe Resent Arrests

Admiral Announces Plans He Is To Make For Fleet's Coming

Marshal Tuan Denounces Peking Government Urging People To Oust Tsao Kun

FIRE IN PEKING?

Shanghai Hit by strong Wind, Rain Storm; Report Says Lu Is Nearing City

MACHINE GUN SQUADS HERE GO TO KAUAI

National Guardsmen Will be sent to Trouble Zone Today

Four Police Among Those Killed; Sheriff Crowell Wounded; Dead Are Left on Roadside As Injured Rushed To Hospital; Arrest Hundreds

PUBLIC BATHS MANAGEMENT IS UNDER FIRE

OAHU WATER PROVES BEST IN THE WORLD

FREITAS 'GETS THREE YEARS FOR ASSAULT

The Voice of Labor
HAWAII'S ONLY WORKING-CLASS NEWSPAPER

For A United Labor Front

Don't Forget To Register!

VOL. III. No. 39

HONOLULU, T. H., THURSDAY, AUGUST 4, 1938

PRICE FIVE CENTS

"THEY EVEN SHOT MEN IN THE BACK"

Nationwide Protests Deluge Poindexter and Washington

Editorial

Editor Coll Does A Fireside Chat — and Burns Himself

"Ripped Their Bodies With Bayonets; Shot Men Picking Up Their Wounded Comrades"

By HARRY KAMOKU
As told to Edward Berman

HILO, Hawaii, Aug. 3rd:—"They shot us down like a

As immigrant communities in the Islands matured, they began to demand higher wages, better working conditions, and collective bargaining. The earliest strikes were essentially wildcat shutdowns initiated by disgruntled workers on individual plantations. However, in 1909, the Japanese labor force organized an island-wide strike on O'ahu that shocked plantation owners and cost the sugar industry a million dollars. The great strike of 1920 was another unsuccessful attempt by Japanese workers to improve wages, although some demands were met. In 1924, violence erupted on Kaua'i during a Filipino strike led by labor activist Pablo Manlapit. Yet in these early years ethnic jealousies between unions were difficult to overcome; the "divide and rule" strategy of plantation owners invariably succeeded in averting strikes. [Hawai'i State Archives]

Thalia and Lt. Thomas Massie became the center of the sensational Massie murder trial, one of the Associated Press's top ten stories of 1932. The famed Chicago defense attorney Clarence Darrow, pictured here at the courthouse with his co-defendants Lt. Massie and Grace Fortesque, the mother of Thalia Massie, argued his last and most ignominious case in Honolulu. [Hawai'i State Archives]

In the early hours of September 13, 1931, two separate incidents were logged by the Honolulu Police Department. A local couple reported being in a near-accident and altercation with a group of local men. One hour later, Thalia Massie, wife of U.S. Navy officer Lt. Thomas Massie, reported being abducted off of a Waikīkī street by a group of local men, beaten, and raped. Police linked both incidents and arrested the owner of the automobile involved in the accident, as well as his four companions. Considering the ethnicity of the victim, her husband's connection to the military, and the sensationalism of the alleged crime,

the five defendants were automatically considered guilty by the haole community. When a multiethnic jury failed to reach a verdict, a mistrial was declared and racial tensions in the city reached a fever pitch.

In January 1932, Joseph Kahahawai awaited retrial on the rape charges. Unexpectedly, he was kidnapped by Lt. Massie, Massie's mother-in-law, Grace Fortesque, and two other sailors; taken to a bungalow in Mānoa; tortured for a confession; and then murdered. Massie and the others were arrested later trying to dispose of the body in the "Blowhole" on O'ahu's southern coast. The subsequent

trial of the Massie group was a courtroom drama that attracted national attention, with famed lawyer Clarnece Darrow representing the defendants. All four were found guilty of manslaughter and sentenced to ten years in prison. Under pressure from Washington, D.C., and the U.S. military, Governor Judd of Hawai'i commuted the sentences to one hour, served with police escort in his offices at 'Iolani Palace. Native Hawaiians and other nonwhite islanders saw the Massie case as representing a dual system of justice based on an institutional racism which mocked the older, prevailing spirit of aloha. The façade of ethnic harmony had been stripped away.

Melting Pot

"Hawai'i's Melting Pot"

1. Hawaiian
2. 'Ehu Hawaiian
3. Japanese
4. Chinese
5. Korean
6. Russian
7. Filipino
8. Portuguese
9. Polish-Russian
10. Hawaiian-German
11. Hawaiian-Chinese
12. Hawaiian-Russian
13. Hawaiian-American
14. Hawaiian-French
15. Hawaiian-Portuguese
16. Hawaiian-Filipino-Chinese
17. Hawaiian-Indian-American
18. Hawaiian-Japanese-Portuguese
19. Hawaiian-Portuguese-American
20. Hawaiian-Spanish-American
21. Hawaiian-German-Irish
22. Hawaiian-Spanish-German
23. Hawaiian-Chinese-American
24. Hawaiian-Portuguese-Irish
25. Hawaiian-Japanese-Indian
26. Hawaiian-Portuguese-Chinese-English
27. Hawaiian-Chinese-German-Norwegian-Irish
28. South Sea (Nauru)-Norwegian
29. African-French-Irish
30. Spanish-Puerto Rican
31. Guamanian-Mexican-French
32. Samoan-Tahitian

By the start of the twentieth century, Hawai'i's multiethnic mixture was applauded by social scientists as a "living laboratory of human relations." Extensive immigration from Asia, the Pacific Islands, Europe, and the Americas to support the sugar plantation economy, and the subsequently high interracial marriage rates, had created a fascinating cultural mosaic popularized as the "Melting Pot." Photographs of young islanders, such as this 1920 portrait of numbered and ethnically identified women, were frequently published as evidence that the Hawaiian Islands were truly the "Crossroads of the Pacific." [Hawai'i State Archives]

All the nostalgic appeal of the Hawaii Calls *radio show is captured in this photo from the 1930s. The lady in the hat is the beloved Hilo Hattie.* [Hawai'i State Archives]

There were millions of Americans who, as children in the 1930s and 1940s, remember tuning in to a radio program named *Hawaii Calls*. They would await that thrilling opening moment when the soft wash of the surf on the beach and the haunting sound of the conch-shell trumpet could be heard. Thoughts of the swaying palms, the sandy beach, the blue sky, and the colorfully costumed Hawaiian singers were stimulated by "the magic of radio." More than anything else, *Hawaii Calls* was responsible for popularizing Hawaiian music in the continental U.S. and in other parts of the world, where it was heard by shortwave radio.

The music played on the program was known as hapa-haole, or half-white, music. These were songs sung in a Hawaiian style consisting of mostly English words with a few Hawaiian words thrown in for spice and color. Some, including "Sweet Leilani" and "My Little Grass Shack," became world famous. The program and its performers presented the kind of Hawaiian entertainment that they felt the outside world wanted to hear. Often the performers sang Hawaiian songs in the Hawaiian language, but the overall emphasis was on the hapa-haole music so popular at the time. Many Hawaiian entertainers got their start on *Hawaii Calls* and later went off to show-business fame on their own.

Today, Hawaiian music is undergoing a renaissance with Hawaiian music of the countryside becoming more popular. Slack-key guitar and Hawaiian folk songs form the major components of concerts given by today's musicians. In Waikīkī nightclubs and at commercial lū'aus for visitors, however, the music tends toward the older hapa-haole songs.

Pineapple

The word pineapple almost automatically evokes an association with Hawai'i, where the growing of pineapples first became a big business. The Hawaiian pineapple was among the most delicious produced anywhere, though it was not indigenous to the Islands. While the Hawaiians brought many plants with them from their homelands, the pineapple was not one of them. The Hawaiians called the pineapple "hala kahiki" meaning "the foreign pandanus," because of its superficial resemblance to the fruit of the pandanus tree.

Commercial pineapple planting in Hawai'i started hesitantly about the middle of the nineteenth century in Kailua-Kona on the Big Island. A variety known as "Wild Kailua" was traded to whaling ships and many tons were sent to the growing towns and settlements in California. But due to a high spoilage rate, the fledgling industry failed.

In 1886, an Englishman, John Kidwell, brought in a variety known as the "Smooth Cayenne." Because of its uniform size and delicious flavor, it is still the standard variety grown today. Since the fruit was too perishable to withstand the long journey to the West Coast, Kidwell realized that the only practical way to enter the American market would be to can the fruit. Though his initial venture failed, he had made a step in the right direction.

In 1899, James D. Dole arrived in Hawai'i. With borrowed capital he established large plantations in central O'ahu near Wahiawā where he built a cannery adjacent to the fields. In 1903, a total of 1,800 cases were packed. Later, the same amount would be packed in minutes. He introduced the Ginaca machine to the canning process. It was an ingenious device that could trim and core pineapples in a single motion, speeding up the preparation of the fruit and leading to the assembly-plant process later initiated at the famed cannery in Iwilei.

By 1950, the number of cases of canned pineapple annually produced in Hawai'i had grown to twenty-four million, constituting eighty percent of the world's output. Pineapple was second only to sugar as Hawai'i's most lucrative agricultural industry, with ten companies and nine canneries employing ten thousand full-time employees. Over seventy thousand acres of land on five islands were being cultivated in pineapple. At the cannery in Iwilei, the ingenious Ginaca machines worked overtime as the fruit moved along assembly lines inspected by island women before canning. Many thousands of young people found temporary work at the canneries during the peak summer season. For visitors to Honolulu, one of the first and memorable sensations was driving past the Iwilei cannery on the way to Waikīkī. The colorful, distinctive pineapple water tower above the cannery was a landmark symbol while the pungent smell of the warm, cooked fruit wafted through the district.

The industry dwindled in size in the face of growing foreign competition, whose costs were much lower and environmental standards less stringent. More than half of Hawai'i's current production is fresh pineapple for local consumption or for tourists to take home.

James Drummond Dole plowing his first pineapple field in 1901 near Wahiawā. Dole is on the right. This field was the beginning of the immense pineapple plantations that cover much of O'ahu's central plateau. Others in the photo include Fred Tracy, and Inez and Muriel Gibson. [Hawaiian Pineapple Company]

Jobs were filled predominantly by women and students during the canning season. [Dole Pineapple Company]

The canning process included many separate steps. [Dole Pineapple Company]

Employees being paid at Waipiʻo Camp, Oʻahu. [Jan K. Ten Bruggencate Collection]

The Honolulu waterfront in 1929 was dominated by the four-year-old Aloha Tower, which rose ten stories over the esplanade for arriving and departing passenger ships. The cement and steel structure contained four bronze clocks, built at the cost of $190,000 each, which weighed seven tons and were guaranteed to keep an accuracy of within thirty seconds per month. A symbol of hospitality, the tower also served as a shoreline beacon, its 5,550-candlepower light visible twenty miles at sea. [Hawai'i State Archives]

(7C-11) HONOLULU FROM THE N.W.

In this early 1930s aerial view of downtown Honolulu looking toward Diamond Head, Aloha Tower (center, right of the smokestacks) still appears as the tallest structure on O'ahu. Honolulu Harbor in the 1930s was increasingly viewed as a strategic outpost in the western defense of the United States. The coastal defense system to protect the harbor included Battery Randolph, hidden in the foliage of Fort DeRussy in Waikiki (to the back of Diamond Head). The U.S. Army positioned mortars at Fort Ruger to protect the vulnerable beaches along the coast. At the tip of Diamond Head, observation bunkers were constructed to watch for an invasion fleet. Fort Armstrong was established at the historic entrance to the harbor (seen at the right). Oil and gas tanks at Iwilei (in the foreground) provided the major reserve for both civilians and military purposes. Even as the United States was building up its defense systems, the empire of Japan was calculating the risks and advantages of an air and naval strike on the island of O'ahu. [Hawai'i State Archives]

Honolulu Star-Bulletin 1st EXTRA

8 PAGES—HONOLULU, TERRITORY OF HAWAII, U.S.A., SUNDAY, DECEMBER 7, 1941—8 PAGES ★ PRICE FIVE CENTS

WAR!

(Associated Press by Transpacific Telephone)

SAN FRANCISCO, Dec. 7.—President Roosevelt announced this morning that Japanese planes had attacked Manila and Pearl Harbor.

OAHU BOMBED BY JAPANESE PLANES

SIX KNOWN DEAD, 21 INJURED, AT EMERGENCY HOSPITAL

Attack Made On Island's Defense Areas

By UNITED PRESS

WASHINGTON, Dec. 7.—Text of a White House announcement detailing the attack on the Hawaiian islands is:

"The Japanese attacked Pearl Harbor from the air and all naval and military activities on the island of Oahu, principal American base in the Hawaiian islands."

Oahu was attacked at 7:55 this morning by Japanese planes.

The Rising Sun, emblem of Japan, was seen on plane wing tips.

Wave after wave of bombers streamed through the clouded morning sky from the southwest and flung their missiles on a city resting in peaceful Sabbath calm.

According to an unconfirmed report received at the governor's office, the Japanese force that attacked Oahu reached island waters aboard two small airplane carriers.

It was also reported that at the governor's office either an attempt had been made to bomb the USS Lexington, or that it had been bombed.

CIVILIANS ORDERED OFF STREETS

The army has ordered that all civilians stay off the streets and highways and not use telephones.

Evidence that the Japanese attack has registered some hits was shown by three billowing pillars of smoke in the Pearl Harbor and Hickam field area.

All navy personnel and civilian defense workers, with the exception of women, have been ordered to duty at Pearl Harbor.

The Pearl Harbor highway was immediately a mass of racing cars.

A trickling stream of injured people began pouring into the city emergency hospital a few minutes after the bombardment started.

Thousands of telephone calls almost swamped the Mutual Telephone Co., which put extra operators on duty.

At The Star-Bulletin office the phone calls deluged the single operator and it was impossible for this newspaper, for sometime, to handle the flood of calls. Here also an emergency operator was called.

HOUR OF ATTACK—7:55 A. M.

An official army report from department headquarters, made public shortly before 11, is that the first attack was at 7:55 a. m.

Witnesses said they saw at least 50 airplanes over Pearl Harbor.

The attack centered in the Pearl Harbor, Army authorities said:

"The rising sun was seen on the wing tips of

ANTIAIRCRAFT GUNS IN ACTION

First indication of the raid came shortly before 8 this morning when antiaircraft guns around Pearl Harbor began sending up a thunderous barrage.

At the same time a vast cloud of black smoke arose from the naval base and also from Hickam field where flames could be seen.

BOMB NEAR GOVERNOR'S MANSION

Shortly before 9:30 a bomb fell near Washington Place, the residence of the governor. Governor Poindexter and Secretary Charles M. Hite were there.

It was reported that the bomb killed an unidentified Chinese man across the street in front of the Schuman Carriage Co. where windows were broken.

C. E. Daniels, a welder, found a fragment of shell or bomb at South and Queen Sts. which he brought into the City Hall. This fragment weighed about a pound.

At 10:05 a. m. today Governor Poindexter telephoned to The Star-Bulletin announcing he has declared a state of emergency for the entire territory.

He announced that Edouard L. Doty, executive secretary of the major disaster council, has been appointed director under the M-Day law's provisions.

Governor Poindexter urged all residents of Honolulu to remain off the street, and the people of the territory to remain calm.

Hundreds See City Bombed

Hundreds of Honolulans who hurried to the top of Punchbowl soon after bombs began to fall, saw spread out before them the whole panorama of surprise attack and defense.

Far off over Pearl Harbor the white sky was polka-dotted with anti-aircraft smoke.

Rolling away from the navy base were billowing clouds of ugly black smoke. Sometimes a burst of flame reddened the black sources of the smoke.

Off from the silver-surfaced depths of the harbor a fist-ful of devastation crossed to battle, smoke pouring from their stacks.

Schools Closed

All schools on Oahu, both public and private, will remain closed until further notice. Edouard L. Doty, territorial director of civilian defense, announced at 11 a. m. today. This does not apply elsewhere in the territory.

Names of Dead and Injured

The city emergency hospital reported at 10:30 a list of 6 killed and 21 injured.

The complete list will be carried later. Here is a partial list:

Peter Lopes, 34, of 2841 Kaimana-hila St., was reported at 2:30 a. m. to be in serious condition from wounds in the upper abdomen.

Bernice Gonveia, 12, 7766 Kalihi St., is suffering from a mangled thigh, lacerations on the right leg and left arm.

A Portuguese girl, unidentified, 18 years old, died on arrival from puncture wounds.

Another victim who died on arrival was Frank Ohashi, 28, 2766 Kamanahi St., from puncture wounds in the chest.

Cecelia Breanby, 31, Mananhui gardens, was released from the hospital after treatment for lacerations.

Three were reported injured and one reported killed from the bomb that fell at Fort and School Sts.

Editorial

HAWAII MEETS THE CRISIS

Honolulu and Hawaii will meet the emergency of war today as Honolulu and Hawaii have met emergencies in the past, calmly and with immediate and complete

Aircraft destroyed on the ground at Ford Island in Pearl Harbor. In the background, the smoke and flames of giant battleships destroyed at their berths. [U. S. Navy–National Archives]

World War II

Pearl Harbor

During the first few minutes of the Pearl Harbor attack, the USS Arizona *took a hit from a 1,760-pound armor-piercing bomb that slammed through the deck. The forward ammunition magazine instantly exploded with a horrific blast that sent a column of black smoke spiraling from the ship. Within nine minutes, as burning oil turned the ocean into an inferno, the USS* Arizona *and 1,177 of her crew sank to the bottom of the harbor.* [U. S. Navy–National Archives]

World War II

The Pearl Harbor disaster ranks as one of the major events in both American and Hawaiian history. Controversy remains as to why our forces were caught so completely off-guard despite numerous indications that trouble with Japan was imminent. Even the Imperial Japanese Admiralty had hardly expected such a complete destruction of America's naval power in the Pacific.

Planes had been detected by radar when they were more than a hundred miles away, but no general alarm was sounded, as the received signal was thought to have been reflected from American carrier-based planes on maneuvers or from a flight of bombers expected from the continental U.S. When the attacking planes came over Kolekole Pass headed toward Pearl Harbor, not an anti-aircraft gun was firing, nor were any fighter planes in the air to challenge them.

In one hour and fifty minutes the attacking carrier-based planes managed to destroy virtually the entire American Pacific Fleet. Eight huge battleships were either sunk or damaged during the Japanese attack. Only the USS *Nevada* managed to get underway, though she too was eventually run aground after a severe bombing attack. Off Ford Island, three light cruisers were seriously damaged; three destroyers and four lesser vessels suffered the same fate as the giants on Battleship Row. Damaged and destroyed American planes, most on the ground, totaled 347. The U.S. military death toll was 2,251.

The Japanese attack on Pearl Harbor, aside from its destructiveness, had an impact on Hawai'i's history almost as great as Captain Cook's arrival 163 years before. Until December 7, 1941, Hawai'i had slumbered on quietly, dominated by its plantation economy and a business establishment almost completely in the hands of a few closely linked corporations. Each major ethnic group kept roughly to its assigned occupational category.

The aftermath of Pearl Harbor, with its tremendous influx of soldiers and workers from the mainland, changed that. Hawai'i's sons, often only one generation removed from the plantations, served in the U.S. military, receiving an invaluable education about the U.S. and other parts of the world. They returned home determined to participate fully in Hawai'i's society.

The USS Arizona *Memorial at Pearl Harbor, built over the hull of the sunken battleship.* [U.S. Navy]

World War II

"Loose Lips Sink Ships" was a constant fear for Hawai'i's military government, which attempted to minimize the flow of sensitive information into the civilian population. All letters handled by the U.S. Post Office were censored for any mention of ship movements, and indecipherable words were cut out. To encourage the entire population to "Serve in Silence," in 1944 a parade was conducted on downtown Hotel Street. Store display windows were decorated with posters and slogans to remind everyone that "Rumors Delay Victory." [U.S. Army Museum of Hawai'i]

A Japanese family returns from internment on the mainland, December 11, 1946. [Hawai'i War Records Depository / University of Hawai'i at Mānoa]

Above: On August 10, 1944, Admiral Nimitz points to the Japanese home islands on a large map of the Western Pacific to an audience of General Douglas MacArthur, President Franklin D. Roosevelt, and Admiral William Healy. Nimitz argued strenuously with maps and intelligence information that fighting the Japanese in the Philippines would be unnecessary. By neutralizing Japan's airbases in the region, the U.S. Navy could instead go on to invade Formosa and launch an attack on Japan. General MacArthur then rose and, speaking without maps or notes, told President Roosevelt that bypassing the Philippines would be politically and militarily disastrous. "American public opinion will condemn you," he finally stated. "And it will be justified." With a re-election campaign only months away, FDR approved MacArthur's highly publicized "return to the Phillipines."

Damage at King and McCully streets, December 7, 1941. [Hawaiʻi War Records Depository / University of Hawaiʻi at Mānoa]

World War II
Hawai'i's Very Special Regiment

[Hawai'i State Archives / Signal Corps U.S. Army]

Left: Hawai'i's 422nd is off to the war in a ceremony at 'Iolani Palace on March 28, 1943. Nisei volunteers in the army spent only a short time at Schofield Barracks's "Tent City" before being shipped out to basic training at Camp Shelby, Mississippi. Recognizing that these young men had family members who wanted to wish them a special aloha before leaving, the military arranged a farewell ceremony at 'Iolani Palace in March of 1943. A huge crowd of friends and relatives watched two thousand new soldiers march smartly down King Street, then assemble on the palace grounds for final speeches, an official photograph, and to receive lei and small envelopes of cash as traditional gifts. The actual date these soldiers were to leave Honolulu for Oakland, California, was a military secret. Several days after the official departure ceremony, they were awakened early and taken by the O'ahu Railway to 'A'ala Park. As they shouldered their heavy duffel bags from the station to the ship docked at the harbor, they expected a quiet farewell from their beloved Islands. However, all the streets were lined with families and friends who had gotten word of the "secret" departure form the "coconut wireless." This unofficial sendoff was an emotional moment they carried with them halfway around the world. [Hawai'i State Archives]

The Japanese attack on Pearl Harbor caused difficulty for America's citizens of Japanese ancestry. Those on the continent were quickly dispossessed and moved to relocation camps. But for the 160,000 Japanese in Hawai'i, most of whom were citizens, internment was impractical. There were not enough ships available to send them to camps on the continent, and it would have been impossible to intern one-third of the entire population of Hawai'i.

Still, the military remained uncomfortable with the possibility of a Japanese invasion of the Hawaiian Islands at the time when the population of Hawai'i was so largely Japanese and there were 1,300 Americans of Japanese Ancestry (AJAs) on duty in Hawai'i's two national guard battalions. To discharge all of the AJAs was a military luxury that could not be afforded at the time. The military's solution was to separate the Japanese contingent, forming the Hawaiian Provisional Infantry Battalion composed of 1,406 Nisei (second-generation Japanese) soldiers. During the Battle of Midway, the soldiers were sent to Camp McCoy in Wisconsin, where they were treated with considerable friendliness by people of the nearby towns. Later, however, they were transferred to Camp Shelby in Mississippi, where racial hostility toward them at times was intense because of their "color." The Hawaiian Provisional Infantry Battalion was renamed the 100th Battalion and, after training, was sent to North Africa and then to Italy.

Later the War Department authorized the formation of an all-AJA fighting unit and put out a call for Hawai'i volunteers in early 1943.

The original appeal was for 1,500 volunteers, but within a month over 9,000 young AJAs flocked to recruitment centers in Hawai'i. Some 2,645 were selected to serve and they formed the core of the 442nd Infantry Regiment. On June 11, 1944, they joined the 100th Battalion north of Rome and eventually absorbed that unit.

The combat record of these young Japanese-Americans is unequalled in the annals of American military history. They fought valiantly in Italy and France. Their casualty rate was three times higher than the average. The combined units won seven Presidential Unit Citations and nearly six thousand other medals were awarded to individual soldiers.

The men of the 442nd returned to Hawai'i as a new kind of citizen. They had traveled; they had seen much, and suffered much. Soon, they would enter politics and help transform Hawai'i into a new and more democratic place with social justice for all and where all men had their say in the decisions that would shape Hawai'i's future.

TWENTIETH CENTURY: 1950–2000

The decade of the 1950s was a transitional period, reflecting the shift from a rural to an urban Island society. Downtown Honolulu, as viewed from Aloha Tower in 1958, still retained the distinctive architectural charm of the Hawaiian style promoted in the early territorial era by C. W. Dickey and Hart Wood. Still visible in this photograph are the domed American Factors building (in the foreground at Fort and Queen streets), the roof of the nineteenth-century historic courthouse on Queen Street, the Alexander Young Hotel (on Bishop Street between King and Hotel streets), and the Damon Building (on the makai–Diamond Head corner of King and Bishop streets). All these historic structures would be replaced by steel-and-glass skyscrapers by the end of the century. [Camera Hawai'i]

1950s

In the late 1950s the Dillingham Corporation began building a large shopping center on a tract of land near Ala Moana Park. The grounds of the future Sears store at Ala Moana Shopping Center were dedicated by Reverend Abraham Akaka in 1958, as the city government braced itself for the enormous impact that the private development would have on sewer lines, water supply, and traffic access. When it was completed, the Ala Moana Shopping Center became the world's largest shopping complex and a local favorite among Island consumers. Within a very short time, many of the department and clothing stores on Fort Street closed, and downtown Honolulu was no longer the center of Island fashion. [Camera Hawai'i]

The Ward Estate, also known as "Old Plantation," remained a rural oasis in the midst of urban development when this photograph was taken in 1952. Built in 1880 by Curtis Perry Ward on thirty acres of land stretching between King Street and the waterfront, the estate was a Honolulu landmark with a lagoon, lush gardens, and thick groves of palm trees. In 1957, the property was condemned by the City and County of Honolulu and purchased for $2,095,000. In September 1958, the public was allowed on the property for a public auction before this piece of history was razed for the construction of a municipal auditorium, convention facility, and sports arena, which were not finished until March 1964. The first event at the concert hall was the Cherry Blossom Festival, while a performance by the Harlem Globetrotters opened the sports arena. The complex was later renamed the Neal Blaisdell Center in honor of the former mayor of the City and County of Honolulu. [Camera Hawai'i]

[Senator Inouye's Office]

After the war, many young Nisei veterans such as Daniel Inouye (above) and Spark Matsunaga (below) returned to the Islands with a zeal for political change. So many Japanese-Americans had sacrificed their lives in the name of freedom in Europe that the survivors were determined to redress the political and economic inequities in Hawai'i, where the "Big Five" were still in control. Revitalizing the Democratic Party and forming important alliances with the local labor movement, these Nisei leaders staged a "Bloodless Revolution" in 1954, seizing control of both houses in the territorial legislature. The domination of the Islands by the sugar oligarchy faded quickly as a new Asian-American middle class emerged "on the make" and with growing political clout.

[Family of Spark Matsunaga]

In the postwar era another tidal wave of change was about to sweep through the Islands, a tsunami of labor unrest and political protest which eventually unseated the territorial powers that had ruled Hawai'i for over forty years. During World War II, the firm hand of martial law prevented any efforts by labor leaders to improve the conditions of workers on sugar plantations. However, after the war the International Longshoremen's and Warehousemen's Union (ILWU), under the leadership of Jack Hall, took aggressive action to organize a united, multicultural front against the "Big Five" oligarchy. In September of 1946, over twenty-one thousand workers on thirty-three plantations went on strike, virtually shutting down the sugar industry. The strike dragged on through October with thousands of pickets, scores of arrests, and threatening accusations that the Islands were controlled by a tyranny of labor unions. Finally, after seventy-nine days, the ILWU was victorious. The plantations' paternal system of providing employees with housing and credit at the company store had ended—workers now earned cash they could spend at their own discretion.

Scenes of unrest at Pier 32 [Bob Ebert]

The ILWU's success was followed by active organizing throughout the plantations and on the waterfronts. By 1947, the union had thirty thousand members—more than any other union in the Islands—and significant political clout. The ILWU worked with the once almost defunct Democratic Party to sponsor territorial office candidates with a favorable stance on labor. When charges of communist infiltration surfaced in 1948, the political struggle over economic justice in Hawai'i attracted national attention.

On May 1, 1949, the storm broke when two thousand ILWU dock workers walked off the job and brought Hawai'i's economy to a standstill. Nothing could enter or leave the Islands, thirty-four thousand people were laid off, businesses closed, and household supplies dwindled. Scenes of labor unrest at Pier 32, or at labor rallies in Honolulu, were common as the dock strike continued for 177 days. Finally, the longshoremen won a wage increase. The era of the "Big Five" oligarchy was clearly coming to an end. [*Bob Ebert*]

Labor rally in Honolulu [Bob Ebert]

Statehood

A newsboy proudly carries the papers headlining statehood. [John Titchen, *Honolulu Star-Bulletin*]

In the 1950s, many islanders saw Hawai'i's territorial status as another stigma of a second-class citizenship under the regime of the sugar oligarchy. Statehood, they believed, would allow full and equal rights under the American flag, including election of a governor, full representation in Congress, and voting for state judges. To demonstrate popular support, in 1954 a "Statehood Roll of Honor" was spread out on Honolulu's Bishop Street. The three-mile-long roll of newsprint extended between King and Hotel streets, and an estimated one hundred-fifty thousand residents signed the petition, which was sent to Washington, D.C. [*Honolulu Advertiser*]

The idea of statehood for Hawai'i originated well before World War II. Technically, statehood had been proposed as early as 1854 in an aborted treaty of annexation that contained a clause calling for eventual statehood. The notion began to be taken seriously by people outside Hawai'i sometime in the early 1950s.

Certainly Hawai'i had taken blows for America, having been attacked in the infamous Pearl Harbor bombing in 1941. Over thirty thousand of its young men and women had served in the armed forces during World War II, and its Nisei regiment, the 442nd, won unparalleled battlefield honors. Ninety percent of Hawai'i's people were full-fledged U.S. citizens and her population of half a million already outnumbered that of some of the other U.S. states.

As early as 1948, the Democratic Party included statehood for Hawai'i in its campaign platform and the Republicans followed suit four years later. The Hawai'i Statehood Commission lobbied actively year after year. Opposition to statehood came from a few southern congressmen and senators, assisted by certain conservative northern legislators. These opponents claimed that Hawai'i was a "non-contiguous" territory and had no place as a state; that the Islands were home to more Communists than any other state in the Union; and so on. In truth, many southern Democrats and conservative legislators of both parties were uncomfortable with the idea of an American state where the majority of citizens were not white and were expected to vote Republican to the detriment of the national political balance.

Unsuccessful statehood bills appeared in Congress in 1947, 1950, and 1953. Alaska was also petitioning to become a state and the admission of either or both states would change the prevailing situation in Congress vis-a-vis Democrats and Republicans. Finally, in 1958, Congressional Delegate Jack Burns, who later became governor, recognized that if Democratic Alaska were allowed statehood first, then Congress would be willing to accept Republican Hawai'i. In June 1958 Alaska became the forty-ninth state.

With the admission of non-contiguous Alaska, some remaining objections to Hawaiian statehood were removed. Congress finally voted for statehood on March 12, 1959. After a plebiscite in which Hawai'i's voters overwhelmingly approved statehood, Hawai'i was admitted on August 21. Ironically, Jack Burns, who had done so much to bring statehood to Hawai'i, was not invited to the signing of the proclamation in Washington, D.C.

Above left: John A. (Jack) Burns, who labored so mightily for statehood and who served as governor from 1962 to 1974. As champion of Japanese-American participation in Island politics, he lived to see his protégé, George Ariyoshi, become the nation's first governor of Japanese ancestry. [Hawai'i State Archives]

Below left: President Dwight David Eisenhower signs the Statehood Act on August 21, 1959. [National Archives]

Post Statehood

James Michener, whose novel Hawai'i *would become a worldwide best-selling saga, on a 1954 visit with Donn Beach, aka Don the Beachcomber. [Phoebe Beach Collection]*

Plantation laborers returning to camp on company trucks, Waipi'o Camp, O'ahu. [Jan K. Ten Bruggencate Collection]

In 1968, when Hawaii Five-O *debuted on CBS, few knew that twelve years and 284 episodes later, it would be the longest-running police show in media history. Part of the recipe for the series' popularity was the on-location filming against the beautiful and exotic scenery of Hawai'i, against which crime stories's unfolded with local personalities often featured in cameo roles. The other reason for the success of the series was its star and producer, Jack Lord, who, as gruff Steve McGarrett, fought a relentless battle against evil. His customary signature ending, "Book 'em, Danno," was viewed in eighty countries, with a weekly audience estimated at more than three hundred million. The show did more to boost Island tourism than any advertising campaign could ever hope to achieve. [*Hawaii Five-O*]*

High Sheriff of the City and County of Honolulu Duke Paoa Kahanamoku. [Hawai'i State Archives]

Duke greets the Queen of England at Honolulu International Airport in 1966. At Duke's right is his wife, Nadine. To the Queen's left is Hawai'i Governor John A. Burns. As Hawai'i's official greeter, Duke Kahanamoku welcomed prominent visitors from all over the world. Duke's outgoing personality made even the most reserved feel at home. Queen Mother Elizabeth of Great Britain was so charmed by the Duke's infectious gaiety that she joined him in an impromptu hula, to the delight of one and all. [Hawai'i Visitors Bureau]

Hilo Hattie teaching visiting statesmen the hula. [Hawai'i State Archives]

The 1980s increase in Japanese visitors to the Islands was a driving force behind the upscale services and products sold in Waikīkī. To capitalize on these free-spending consumers, exclusive stores proliferated in the major tourist shopping centers, including the internationally famous Ala Moana Shopping Center. [Charles Okamura / Honolulu Advertiser]

The Neighbor Islands

Most of the significant events during the last two centuries of Hawaiian history have occurred on the island of Oʻahu. There was good reason for this: the island's excellent harbor facilities made the port of Honolulu the shipping and business hub of the archipelago.

During the long centuries before the arrival of Captain Cook, each major island was a separate and equally important kingdom. The population of the islands was fairly evenly distributed. (In contrast, the island of Oʻahu today is home to over seventy percent of the state's total population.) Pre-contact history centered on civil wars and territorial disputes among district chiefs. Sometimes powerful chiefs invaded other islands. Important battles were fought on the Big Island and Maui and it was through such fighting that Kamehameha conquered his rivals and unified the islands.

Once the kingdom was united, it needed a central place of authority. The capital had previously been at Kailua-Kona on the island of Hawaiʻi and later at Lahaina on Maui. However, it soon became apparent that the government needed to keep abreast of the fast-moving developments that were affecting the kingdom. It also needed to monitor the arrival and departure of vessels once trade began. Honolulu, with its growing importance as a business and population center, was the obvious choice. In the early 1900s, Oʻahu's importance was fortified by the establishment of military bases there.

For the most part, the post-contact histories of each island have mirrored that of Oʻahu. On each island, immigrants from different countries were recruited to work in the cane fields to meet the demands of the growing sugar industry. On each island, a multicultural society emerged as the immigrants' descendants intermarried and their children received an American education in the public schools. Calvinist missionaries proselytized to Hawaiians devastated by Western diseases, and built churches and schools on all the islands.

Although the similarities were striking, there were some differences in the history of the neighbor islands. They were impacted less by World War II, though there were important training bases on the Big

In 1939, this section of the Big Island's Hāmākua Coast was heavily planted with taro. Taro root was the staple of the Hawaiian diet when mashed into poi. It was as important to the Hawaiians as was the potato to the Irish. [Baker–Van Dyke Collection]

The Neighbor Islands

Island and Maui. Tsunamis, earthquakes, and hurricanes always impacted the neighbor islands—particularly Kaua'i and the Big Island—much harder than O'ahu and Maui, which have been left relatively untouched.

Maui's origins are mythical. The island is named after the Polynesian demigod Māui, who, according to legend, pulled the Hawaiian Islands from the bottom of the sea with his fishhook and slowed the sun's movement across the sky so that there would be more time for drying tapa cloth. Lahaina became an important rest and recreation center for the whalers. While the visitor industry quickly expanded on O'ahu with the development of Waikīkī, Maui only developed a large-scale resort industry in the 1970s with the development of the Ka'anapali area.

Ranching on the Big Island became a major industry compared to the few small ranches on O'ahu and even smaller industries on Maui and Kaua'i. In the early 1920s, hotels were built on the Big Island to accommodate visitors who were coming to view the volcanoes, but it was not until the recent development of the Kohala Coast that tourism became important. The influence of Kīlauea Volcano has shaped the Big Island, which is culturally unlike any other part of the state.

Even today, Kaua'i is referred to as the "Separate Island," because of its relative isolation from the other islands and the fact that it was the last island to become part of the kingdom of Hawai'i. Its residents are proud of their unique customs.

On Ni'ihau, seventeen miles west of Kaua'i's southwestern shore, 160 pure-Hawaiian inhabitants speak Hawaiian as their first language. Known as the "Forbidden Island," it remained an isolated pocket of old Hawai'i until the early 1990s, when helicopter tours began to land on deserted stretches of the seventy-two-square-mile island. The Robinson family has owned Ni'ihau for more than 130 years.

Moloka'i, known always as the "Lonely Island," has so far escaped the state's economic growth. Of its approximately 7,404 residents, many are Hawaiian or part-Hawaiian; and a quiet life of fishing, farming, and hunting still predominates. For long centuries, Moloka'i's kahunas (priests of the ancient Hawaiian religion) were feared for their great powers. Kalaupapa, on the island's north shore, is the site of the former facility housing people with Hansen's disease.

Lāna'i, known as the "Pineapple Island," was once the world's largest source of pineapples. Pineapple now grows only on one hundred acres. Two upscale resorts have replaced pineapple as the backbone of the local economy.

At one time, the neighbor islands were noted as places where a more leisurely life resembling old Hawai'i could be found—places where the urban hustle and bustle of Honolulu could be left behind. In the wake of economic and population growth and inadequate infrastructure, however, their tranquility and laid-back lifestyle are being threatened.

A scene of downtown Hilo area taken in 1878. On April 1, 1946, Hilo's waterfront area was devastated by a giant tidal wave which caused many fatalities and enormous damage. Disaster struck again on May 23, 1960, when a tsunami destroyed much of downtown Hilo. Waves in Hilo Bay reached thirty-five feet, with water washing inland as far as Kīlauea Avenue and Keawe Street. [Baker–Van Dyke Collection]

The Neighbor Islands

The growth of the sugar industry on Maui acted as a catalyst for urban development. Wailuku was becoming the island's commercial center when this photograph was taken in 1905, showing ʻĪao Valley in the background (top). A new courthouse opened in 1907, making Wailuku the island's governmental headquarters as well. [Bishop Museum]

Urbanization, roads, and automobiles not only transformed Oʻahu, but touched all of the islands as the agricultural industry churned out profits from sugar, pineapple, and coffee. Lahaina's reputation as a whaling port faded into the past as Front Street hummed with traffic in the 1920s. By the 1930s, Lahaina had a population of seven thousand, most of whom worked for west Maui sugar and pineapple operations. [Nakamoto Art Studios]

Loading cattle at Kailua-Kona near the American Factors warehouse. [Hawai'i State Archives]

One of the most distinctive aspects of ranching on the island of Hawai'i was hoisting cattle onto ships at Kawaihae, Kīholo, and Kailua-Kona. The paniolo drove the herds down to the beach, and then out into the ocean, tied to boats where they were lifted aboard one by one. Passengers had to wait on shore until the cattle were safely loaded before they were allowed to board the interisland steamers. [Baker–Van Dyke Collection]

The Neighbor Islands

Madame Pele: The Volcano Goddess

The first Volcano House at Kīlauea Crater opened in 1861 as a grass-thatched building made from ōh'ia wood. In 1877, a sturdier wooden hotel was constructed which many years later would be used as the Volcano Arts Center and moved to the nearby grounds of the Hawai'i Volcanoes National Park Visitor Center. In 1883, the Wilder Steamship Company purchased the unique hostelry. In 1895, the Volcano House was purchased by famed owner "Uncle George" Lycurgus, a Greek immigrant and fervent royalist who had been jailed earlier in the year for participating in the Wilcox Rebellion. "Uncle George" began his long love affair with Kīlauea Crater and the goddess Pele, whose eruptions in the first part of the century made the Volcano House a thriving business. A new, larger and more luxurious hotel, was constructed and stood until it was destroyed by fire in 1940. On the grounds of the Volcano House at the edge of Kīlauea Crater, visitors enjoyed the panoramic view of the world's most active volcanic crater with the magnificent vista of the world's largest mountain, Mauna Loa, in the background. The sights, sounds, and tastes of Hawai'i comprised an exotic excursion which was an unforgettable adventure when tourism was still in its infancy. [Library of Congress]

The series of eruptions of Kīlauea Volcano in the first half of the century were spectacular demonstrations of the power of nature that drew visitors from around the world. One of the most frightening series began in 1924 when the Kīlauea caldera cracked, making the "lake of fire" visible for many years in Pele's legendary home of Halema'uma'u Crater. As the lava vanished, it came into contact with underwater streams, which caused a tremendous explosion. Within moments the crater doubled its size as volcanic bombs were hurled into the air so fast that the friction caused lighting to appear in the skies above the crater. As a gigantic cloud of steam billowed out of the earth, Volcano House shook so violently that many believed it would fall into the crater. The Hawai'i Volcanoes National Park was evacuated for several weeks before visitors were allowed back in May 1924 to gape at the devastation and to be photographed in front of the incredible cauliflower cloud. Two years later, on April 18, 1926, another lava flow destroyed the Hawaiian fishing village of Ho'ōpūloa on the southwest Kona coast. [Baker–Van Dyke Collection]

Rites of Ancient Hawaiian Societies at Kīlauea, 1926. [Baker–Van Dyke Collection]

Destruction of the Hawaiian fishing village of Hoʻōpūloa as the lava nears the sea, April 18, 1926. [Baker–Van Dyke Collection]

EXTRA
TIDAL WAVES CRASH HILO

Honolulu Star-Bulletin

20 PAGES—HONOLULU, T. H., U. S. A., MONDAY, APRIL 1, 1946—20 PAGES

★★★ AIRPLANE DELIVERY ON ISLANDS OTHER THAN OAHU 7¢ PRICE ON OAHU 5¢

LATE NEWS FINAL

Some of the Damage Done By the Waves At the Ala Wai Yacht Harbor

The Sea As It Receded At Waikiki Near the Elks Club. Note Bare Reef.

The Water Receded In Nuuanu Stream. Note the Spectators

The Ala Wai, Makai of Kalakaua and Looking Toward Kaimuki

20 Dead Reported In The Territory And Toll May Grow

The unconfirmed death toll in today's tidal waves at noon today was:

At Hilo, 10 dead and many more feared dead.

On Oahu, 9 reported dead with others missing.

On Kauai, 1 dead, 4 missing.

No deaths reported on Molokai, Maui or Lanai.

Damage is extensive on all islands everywhere and may run into hundreds of thousands of dollars.

Three babies, children of Mr. and Mrs. Haakee of Kalama bay, were the first officially reported deaths as a result of this morning's tidal wave, police said. Three were reported dead at Kahana, two at Waianae and one at Koko Head.

It is believed that the deaths are occurring from raging waters that are resulting and causing cars to overturn on main highways on Oahu.

Up to late this morning the emergency hospital and Queen's hospital reported that casualties are streaming in with injuries, some of which are small, others which are serious.

Circumstances surrounding the deaths have not been determined at this time, police reported.

All available police were called to duty this morning to render aid to Oahu residents, stricken in this morning's tidal wave, Police Chief W. A. Gabrielson reported.

In addition, Boy Scout officials said all scouts and sea scouts may be released from school classes to assist in the emergency.

By DOUGLAS BOSWELL
HILO, Hawaii, April 1. (By Radiophone)—The most destructive tidal wave in the history of Hawaii flattened most of the business district along Kamehameha Ave. in both Hilo and Waiakea today, causing damage running well up into the millions.

No one could determine how many lives were lost, but at least 10 were dead in Hilo and word was received that Laupahoehoe on the Hamakua coast that night mainland

Turn to Page 4, Column 4

Victims Of Tidal Wave!

Call the Red Cross, 3471, for assistance if you urgently need it. This is the call night and day—3471.

The Water's Power Moved Concrete Blocks Used As Anchors

Wrecked Boats At the Yacht Harbor, Near Kalakaua Ave.

The Two Pictures Above Show More Wreckage At the Yacht Harbor

Aleutian Quake Is Blamed

SEATTLE, April 1. (P)—An earthquake of major proportions, which was recorded on seismographs today, was believed by Howard A. Coombs, professor of geology at the University of Washington, to have occurred somewhere in the vicinity of the Aleutian Islands.

He estimated that the shock was about 1,600 miles from Seattle. It could have caused heavy damage if it had occurred in a well populated area, he said.

The first shock was recorded on the university seismograph 4:04 a. m. Pacific standard time (1:46 a. m. HCT), and the shocks continued for hours.

No reports have been received here of the shock being felt in the Aleutians.

The tidal wave is the result of a "world shaking submarine earthquake" which probably took place off the Aleutian islands more than 2,000 miles from Hawaii, Dr. Thomas A. Jaggar, volcanologist, told The Star-Bulletin.

Dr. Jaggar, who ruled out the possibility of an undersea volcanic eruption, said such disturbances were common at this time of the year, usually following the equinox, which occurred March 21.

According to tables compiled by Dr. Jaggar, the first wave struck Oahu at 7 a. m., the next at 7:07 and a third at 7:16.

That if the naval perhaps for disturbances of this kind," Dr. Jaggar said.

"The earthquake unquestionably is a movement of the sea bottom after it would not have been felt here," he added.

No Authentic Reports Of Second Waves

As this edition of The Star-Bulletin went to press there were persistent but absolutely unconfirmed reports that a second tidal wave was expected.

These reports had alarmed various island communities, especially Hilo.

Dr. T. A. Jaggar and others pointed out that there is no reason to expect a second tidal wave onshore there is a second earthquake. In the far Aleutians or elsewhere, and such a quake is a matter of pure conjecture.

ICKES' COLUMN

Tidal waves occur in all oceans but are especially prevalent in the Pacific, which contains more regions of volcanic activity than anywhere else on earth. When earthquakes occur under the sea bottom, they often cause the formation of fast-moving waves that travel rapidly outward. At sea, these waves are hardly distinguishable from normal ocean waves, but as they approach land they may build up, inundating coastal areas and washing away everything in their path. Hawai'i has often suffered devastation from tidal waves, or tsunamis as they are called in Japan. On each occasion, the loss of lives and property damage were greatest on the Big Island, though destruction was considerable elsewhere in the Islands. [Hawai'i State Archives]

Laupāhoehoe was an important settlement in 1880 partly because it was a convenient place to load passengers and cargo on awaiting offshore ships. In 1946 a tidal wave washed over Laupahoehoe Point, killing several school children and marking the decline of the community as a population center. [Baker–Van Dyke Collection]

The Neighbor Islands

Hurricane 'Iniki

As 'Iniki sped towards the Islands, it was headed toward O'ahu, but damage to O'ahu was relatively light—$25.7 million—confined mostly to the Wai'anae Coast on O'ahu's northwestern shore. Although Waikīkī Beach disappeared under turbulent seas during the storm, Honolulu was spared major destruction. If the hurricane had hit Hawai'i's most populated and urbanized island full force, the result may have been catastrophic.

Instead, Hurricane 'Iniki turned slightly north, battering Kaua'i on September 11, 1992, with sustained winds of 145 miles per hour and gusts of up to 227 mile per hour Eight people died of storm-related causes, 332 were injured, 21,000 homes were damaged, and more than a billion dollars' damage to property, businesses, and city and state infrastructures was done. Eight thousand of Kaua'i's fifty thousand people were left homeless. Agricultural losses were estimated at $150 million.

Natural disasters such as Hurricane 'Iniki show the vulnerability of the Hawaiian archipelago to the forces of nature. In addition to hurricanes, there have been numerous volcanic eruptions on the Big Island, particularly since 1983, causing massive uncontrollable lava flows. Fortunately, there has been no loss of life, although villages and subdivisions have been abandoned as a result of the flows. On the optimistic side, new lands, and even a new Hawaiian island, are being created by Madame Pele's volcano.

Mankind has also been a threatening force to the islands. Hawai'i has the highest number of endangered (264) and threatened (9) species of flora and fauna of any of the states.

Weather details, A4		Scenes from the hurricane on Oahu. PAGE A2	Hawaiian Electric says damage to system slight. PAGE A3
		How to find help now that Hurricane Iniki is over. PAGE A3	Waikiki was dark and dreary. PAGE A4
Mostly fair with occasional showers.		Storm brings back gas lines to Oahu. PAGE A3	Hurricane Iniki's path of destruction. PAGE A4

The Honolulu Advertiser

Aloha! September 12, 1992   Final Edition   On Oahu 35¢

INIKI'S MADNESS

Kauai ravaged; Waianae coast hit hard; flooding in Waikiki

Advertiser Staff and News Services

Hurricane Iniki smashed into the northern Hawaiian Islands yesterday, ravaging the island of Kauai and forcing thousands to flee their homes in the face of fearsome winds and destructive storm surf that surged into beachfront homes and luxury hotels.

There was no loss of life reported and damage on populous Oahu was much less severe than anticipated.

Several injuries were reported on Kauai, where the rake of hurricane winds flattened buildings, bowled down trees and caused major structural damage to many buildings in the business and government center of Lihue.

Damage on Kauai was "just mind-boggling " and "as far as the eye can see," according to Civil Defense officials in Honolulu .

Advertiser Kauai Bureau Chief Jan TenBruggencate reported by radio last night that as many as a third of Kauai's homes suffered severe damage and that destruction was visible everywhere.

In addition to torrential rains and winds gusting well in excess of 100 mph, coastal areas were battered by towering storm surf.

Many Kauai residents opted to stay in shelters last night rather than attempt to make it back to their homes, or what was left of them, TenBruggencate reported.

By contrast, damage on populous Oahu was much less than had been expected . Residents along the Leeward Coast reported substantial flooding, surf damage and lost roofs. Waikiki hotels saw storm waves sweep into their lobbies and across streets in the resort center.

But the true devastation was clear on Kauai, which is still in recovery from the much-less- powerful Hurricane Iwa a decade ago.

Debris littered the roads, power poles and trees were down and even substantial government buildings were ravaged. Because travel and communication were nearly impossible, there was no clear idea of the extent of the damage, the governor's office said last night.

Gov. John Waihee declared the entire state a major disaster area last night because of the direct impact on Kauai and the severe weather conditions caused by Iniki. That declaration clears the way for various rebuilding loans and grants and helps speed the process of possible federal relief.

It was the most powerful hurricane in the Hawaiian Islands this century, said Bob Sheets, director of the National Hurricane Center in Coral Gables, Fla. He said Iniki was about as strong as Hurricane Andrew, which roared through the Bahamas, South Florida and Louisiana last month.

While the digging-out process is just beginning for Kauai, most residents on Oahu face today knowing that they had been spared fearsome destruction and grateful that their time of tension had ended.

Before dawn broke over Oahu yesterday with its gray panorama , a heavy humidity and the smell of sea in the air, an eerie siren wailed out its warning at 5:30 a.m.

Within minutes, residents rushed to their cars and created traffic jams around stores and gas stations. Others taped windows and cleared yards of loose objects. Containers were filled with water.

Businesses and schools closed and workers were told to stay home, where radio and television stations held captive audiences. As many as 26,000 fled to shelters, while others hunkered at home.

The waiting game had begun.

By 11 last night Iniki was weakening and moving north, away from the Islands. The weather bureau had downgraded warnings for Kauai and the rest of the Islands, but warned that occasional heavy showers and local flooding

The damage on Kauai was 'mind-boggling'

remained possible.

Forecasters tabbed Iniki as a Category 4 storm , one short of the "catastrophic" category 5. Hurricane Iwa, by contrast, was a Category 1 hurricane.

On Oahu, wave-driven water washed across Farrington Highway in Makaha and in Kalia Road in Waikiki.

Kalanianaole Highway was blocked off, water was reportedly coming over the highway at Maunalua Bay Beach Park.

At Haleiwa, about 1 p.m., a 30-foot sailboat trying to come into the harbor through high surf went aground on a reef. The people aboard reportedly escaped without injury.

Between 300 and 400 people took shelter at the baggage area of Honolulu Airport.

Two companies of National Guard troops were activated to help evacuation of residents along the Waianae Coast and on Kauai.

Navy ships at Pearl Harbor were sent to sea to ride out the storm. Hordes of tourists were sent away from their beachfront hotels in Waikiki.

"Clear the area immediately! This area is closed," Honolulu police called from their Cushman scooters at 11:20 a.m., as they used sirens and horns to push through crowds reluctant to leave Kalakaua Avenue's shorefront sidewalks.

The impact on Oahu was due to strong wind feeding the storm from the east, said meteorologist Tom Heffner of the National Weather Service.

U.S. Sen. Dan Inouye announced yesterday

he had sought to put into motion federal emergency disaster readiness and preparedness measures.

Inouye said the Federal Emergency Management Agency (FEMA) assured him that emergency disaster operations were focused on Iniki as early as 2:30 a.m. yesterday.

Some 27 federal agencies, including the Defense Department, were prepared to assist.

Mayor Frank Fasi and Waihee were in contact with the White House, advising the president that the Islands would likely need major relief help.

Waihee said he received assurances of help from Bush and federal disaster and military officials even before Hurricane Iniki ripped into Hawaii.

Army Secretary Michael Stone assured Waihee that "all military assets including supplies, equipment and manpower would be available to the state," spokesperson Carolyn Tanaka said.

The storm developed to the south early in the week and was expected to move northwest parallel to the island chain before it changed course late Thursday.

Forecasters feared Iniki could be much more destructive than Hurricane Iwa, a Category 1 storm that caused $216 million damage to Hawaii in November 1982.

Hurricane Andrew, the nation's costliest natural disaster, swept over the Bahamas, south Florida and coastal Louisiana last month, killing more than 50 people and flattening thousands of homes. The Pacific island of Guam, 3,800 miles west of Hawaii, was hit by Typhoon Omar on Aug. 29.

Incoming flights with tourists from the Mainland continued to arrive at Honolulu International Airport.

(Advertiser staff members Jan TenBruggencate, Kevin Dayton, David Waite, Jon Yoshishige, Stu Glauberman, John Strobel, Jerry Burris and the Associated Press contributed to this story.)

Neighborhood youths stand in the splash zone as storm surf crashes below Pupu Place in Ewa.   Advertiser photo by Gregory Yamamoto

Floodwaters cover parts of Ala Moana Beach Park and Magic Island yesterday.   Advertiser photo by T. Umeda

Two Kauai boaters swim for their lives

By Jan TenBruggencate

MANA, KAUAI Two Kauai boaters were forced to abandon their fishing boat and swim for their lives in crashing surf yesterday.

The two, Terry Teves and Chris Kam, were returning from a fishing trip with a good catch yesterday morning but found that hurricane-generated surf had closed all Kauai harbors.

An air traffic controller at the Pacific Missile Range Facility heard their emergency CB call and guided them toward the missile base, where there appeared to be a calm area.

Vida Mossman, public information officer at the missile range, said its helicopters had been stored for the storm, but crews rushed to prepare one for an emergency launch.

Mossman said one of the boats engines died as it powered through the stormy ocean.

The control tower made visual contact with the 25-foot boat, the Nalani L. and guided it to within 250 yards from shore.

The men abandoned their ship and started swimming not knowing that a helicopter had just become air borne.

The two, both strong swimmers, made it through the surf onto the beach fronting the missile range without the helicopter's help. Mossman reported both were in good condition.

What's Inside

3 sections, 32 pages

Ann Landers	A8
Classified Ads	C6-16
Comics	A12
Crossword	A12
Editorials	A10
Entertainment, films	A7-9
Global Briefs	B1
Horoscope	A12
Letters to the editor	A11
Money section	B2-4
Obituaries	C5
Religion news	A5-6
Sports section	C1-5
Stocks	B2
Television	A8

Hurricane 'Iwa struck O'ahu and Kaua'i in November of 1982, resulting in one death and $250 million in damage. During this natural disaster, islanders braced themselves against sustained winds clocked at 65 mph, with gusts up to 117 mph. [Honolulu Advertiser]

Hurricane 'Iniki was an unexpected visitor that brought death and destruction in September of 1992 as it surged over the leeward coast of O'ahu and slammed head-on into Kaua'i with sustained winds of 92 mph and gusts up to an extraordinary 143 mph. Four people were killed and over a thousand injured in the most devastating storm of the century. Total damage was estimated at $1.6 billion, crippling Kaua'i's economy for years. [Bruce Asato / Honolulu Advertiser]

The Hawaiian Renaissance

One of the most important political and social developments in recent Hawaiian history was the emergence in the 1970s of the Hawaiian Renaissance, which later evolved into the quest for Hawaiian Sovereignty. It was expressed culturally, in a renewed interest in Hawaiian traditions, including hula, music, history, literature, and crafts; politically, in demands for economic and social changes to correct past historical injustices; and socially, in renewed pride in being Hawaiian.

It brought to a halt the decline of Hawaiian culture that had proceeded practically unabated since contact with the West began, during which time Hawaiians experienced the tragic consequences of massive population decimation caused by foreign diseases, loss of political and social power, and heavy influxes of non-Hawaiian peoples to the Islands.

Hawaiian cultural revivals had occurred before. Under King David Kalākaua, hula and many other aspects of the ancient culture were rescued from near oblivion. When Kalākaua included sacred hulas and chants as part of his coronation celebration, they seemed almost a lost art form. By presenting hula in the style he did, he shocked the stuffier members of Honolulu's society.

Kalākaua's attempt at cultural revival was motivated by his sincere interest in the songs, chants, legends, and dances of his people, which he considered the expression of true nationhood. He was also very much aware of the declining Hawaiian participation in government, and the demoralization of the Hawaiians due to the impact of Western ways and the contempt with which the increasingly dominant foreigners viewed the native culture.

Kalākaua recognized the urgent need to instill a sense of pride in his people and an appreciation for the accomplishments of their ancestors. He felt that with increased self-respect, the Hawaiian people would once more assume their rightful place, governing their land and reversing the disastrous population decline. During Kalākaua's time, many Hawaiians had lost the will to survive, and a shockingly low birth rate was reducing their numbers. When Kalākaua died, his sister Lili'uokalani attempted to continue the revival, but the overthrow of the Hawaiian monarchy shortly after she inherited the throne dealt this revival a fatal blow.

Sporadic attempts at revival continued to be made thereafter, though they were usually restricted to a particular aspect of the ancient culture. Duke Kahanamoku stimulated worldwide enthusiasm for Hawai'i's national sport, surfing. A similar revival of outrigger canoe racing occurred in the early 1900s, when it had become an almost forgotten activity. There were also attempts at setting up Hawaiian cultural centers like Ulu Mau Village, where the ancient arts could be practiced and the old way of life revived. Though the village flourished during the 1950s and 1960s, such projects often encountered public indifference.

In contrast the Hawaiian Renaissance sustained and grew, perhaps influenced by the civil rights and anti-war movements during the time. Perhaps it was a reaction to excessive economic development and urbanization of the Islands. It is difficult to pinpoint any single event that gave rise to the movement. It may have happened simply because its time had come.

The Renaissance quickly became an important force in the Islands and early on its political significance was felt. The navy bombing of Kaho'olawe was scaled down and reparation bills were presented in Congress. Economic plans had to consider the rights of people to the land. In significant ways the Renaissance touched the lives of all Hawai'i's residents with many of the old values and customs being appreciated and practiced openly again.

The Hawaiian Renaissance

Hula

After King Kalākaua's aborted revival of the ancient dances, the hula tended to drift into a pallid imitation of itself—a dance popular in nightclubs catering to tourists or in South Seas movies starring blonde hula maidens dressed in cellophane "grass" skirts. The Hawaiian Renaissance helped rescue this noble art form from degradation. Today the Islands resonate with the dedicated energy of hula schools, which strive to practice the art with authenticity and heart.

Many of these hālau, or schools, headed by kumu hula or masters of hula, teach strict versions of the ancient sacred hulas and chants. Hula is a rigorous discipline and only the most dedicated last. There was also an upsurge of interest in men's hula, a separate set of specific and very vigorous dances.

Modern masters of hula teach the old ways, the transitional styles of Kalākaua's time, the steps and changes introduced during the popularity of "tourist" hula in the thirties and forties, and even add their own innovations. Hula is now alive and evolving, and inspires wherever it is seen. The annual Merrie Monarch Festival, named in honor of His Majesty King Kalākaua, and held every April on the Big Island, is Hawai'i's most prestigious hula competition.

When Hōkūle'a came to visit Hilo after her epic voyage to Tahiti and back, the turnout was enormous as Big Islanders flocked to welcome her. Here dancers perform ancient hulas in honor of the great ship, pride and joy of the Hawaiian people. [Alexis Higdon]

The Hawaiian Renaissance

Hōkūleʻa

The ancient, sacred sands of Kualoa on the windward side of Oʻahu were chosen to be one of Hōkūleʻa's landing sites. With the ceremonial blowing of the pū, or conch, thousands of people waded into the sea to greet the canoe and her crew with an outpouring of aloha. Ceremonial chanting and festivities on the beach celebrated the outstanding contributions that the Hōkūleʻa and her crewmembers made to restoring Hawaiian pride. [Ron Jett / *Honolulu Advertiser*]

When the Hōkūleʻa returned to Hawaiʻi from its historic transpacific voyage, thousands of people welcomed the canoe, first at Magic Island and then at other sites. Here at Kualoa Park in Kāneʻohe Bay a flotilla of sailboats, fishing vessels, rowboats, surfers, and outrigger canoes formed a symbolic lei of aloha around the magnificent canoe. [David Yamada / *Honolulu Advertiser*]

The Hawaiian Renaissance

Hōkūleʻa

Of all the recent manifestations of the Hawaiian Renaissance, no one event has had a more dramatic effect than the voyage of the *Hōkūleʻa*, a replica of the ancient double-hulled migration canoes that brought the first Polynesian inhabitants to Hawaiʻi a thousand years ago. *Hōkūleʻa* means "star of gladness." It is the Hawaiian name often attributed to Arcturus, Hawaiʻi's zenith star, which led the sixty-foot-long canoe home after its successful 1976 voyage to Tahiti. Guided by traditional Polynesian navigational methods, *Hōkūleʻa* reopened a highway on the sea once traveled by similar splendid vessels in the golden age of Polynesian voyaging.

Centuries before European settlers founded colonies on America's eastern shores, Hawaiʻi's earliest pioneers had mastered the navigation of earth's largest ocean, bringing with them to Hawaiʻi a wide range of domesticated plants and animals. The voyage of *Hōkūleʻa* was, in a sense, a time machine, journeying into the past to recreate a saga as basic to the beginnings of Hawaiʻi as the voyage of the *Mayflower* was to the founding of the United States.

Hōkūleʻa and her crew of seventeen arrived in Tahiti to a welcome perhaps then unrivalled in Tahiti's history. Twenty-five thousand or more Tahitians crowded the shoreline of Papeete's harbor to celebrate the accomplishment of their Hawaiian brothers. When the magnificent sailing canoe returned to Hawaiʻi, the crew received a joyous reception by thousands of cheering people. This successful voyage reawakened a deep pride among Hawaiians in the accomplishments of their ancestors, a people who could build a giant sailing vessel using only wooden, bone, and stone tools, and navigate the vast Pacific employing only the stars and other natural signs as guides.

Hōkūleʻa became the visible symbol of everything encompassed in the words "Hawaiian Renaissance." After her return from Tahiti, *Hōkūleʻa* was used as a floating classroom. Elementary and high school students were taken aboard to study how their ancestors navigated and survived on the open ocean in an age when metal tools and electronic instruments were unknown. A planned second trip to Tahiti was aborted only five hours after departure on March 16, 1978, when the *Hōkūleʻa* capsized in rough seas south of Molokaʻi. One crewman, surfer Eddie Aikau, was lost when he left the overturned ship in an attempt to paddle his surfboard to Lānaʻi for help.

The triumph of *Hōkūleʻa* has endured. Her maiden voyage stirred the imaginations of people all over the world. By the mid-1990s the *Hōkūleʻa* had completed five trans-Pacific voyages. On May 13, 1995, the *Hōkūleʻa* finished its first voyage with a flotilla of Polynesian voyaging canoes. *Hōkūleʻa* was joined by two other Hawaiian crafts, as well as a New Zealand Maori canoe and two Cook Island canoes. The motorless boats successfully sailed from Tahiti and the Marquesas to Hawaiʻi using the techniques of wayfinding navigation. For the first time, one of the voyaging vessels, *Hawaiʻiloa*, was constructed primarily of traditional materials.

One of America's most unusual bicentennial projects was the voyage of Hōkūleʻa, a replica of the ancient Polynesian double-hulled migration canoes that brought the first Polynesians to these Islands more than a thousand years ago. The Polynesian Voyaging Society's project was especially fitting as Hawaiʻi's contribution to the 1976 national bicentennial celebration because it symbolizes the uniqueness and exotic heritage of America's only oceanic state. Centuries before European settlers founded colonies on America's eastern shores, Hawaiʻi's earliest settlers had mastered the navigation of the earth's largest ocean, bringing with them the full range of their domesticated plants and animals to start a new life in a new land. [Alexis Higdon]

The Hawaiian Renaissance

Hawaiian Music

There was a time when one could tune in to almost any Honolulu radio station and hear Hawaiian music. By 1970, only one station still consistently played Hawaiian music. Young musicians had lost interest in the old Hawai'i style; they preferred rock music from the mainland. Today, Hawai'i's younger people, particularly those of Hawaiian ancestry, learn older-style Hawaiian music, including the ancient chants, the "hapa-haole" music of the thirties and forties, and today's folk-oriented styles. Reggae, the music of another island people, has also become popular. A Caribbean beat is blended with Hawaiian music to form the "Jawaiian" genre; its name is a combination of the words "Jamaica" and "Hawaiian."

Traditional Hawaiian instrumental music owes its unique sound to the slack-key guitar style. To this style, young Hawaiian musicians have added new instruments and incorporated elements of standard popular music to derive a sound that is innovative but distinctly Hawaiian. New songs reflect a yearning for the simplicity of the old ways and a concern for what is being done to the land.

Eddie Kamae of the Sons of Hawai'i, prominent in Hawaiian music. [Alexis Higdon]

Gabby Pahinui, one of the greats of today's Hawaiian music scene and a musical pioneer of the Hawaiian Renaissance. [Alexis Higdon]

George Helm, talented Hawaiian musician/singer who became passionately involved with the issues of "aloha 'āina" (love for the land) and the misuse of Kaho'olawe. His mysterious disappearance at sea while returning from Kaho'olawe to Maui on a surfboard after having searched for other activists whom he feared were marooned there was a sad loss to all Hawaiians. He was a sensitive, articulate, and gentle man, deeply concerned about the future of these Islands. [Alexis Higdon]

Auntie Genoa Keawe, one of the greats of Hawaiian music. She was famed for her falsetto renditions of the old classics and the sensitivity of her interpretations of Hawai'i's songs. [Alexis Higdon]

The Hawaiian Renaissance

Aloha 'Aina (Love of the Land)

One unfortunate result of the Hawaiians' basic generosity of spirit, which viewed land as coming from the gods and belonging to everyone to be used in trust, was that over the years most of Hawai'i's most valuable land became separated from Hawaiian ownership. Because they lived in a cooperative village social structure, Hawaiians in the olden times had only a vague concept of private property. Thus, it was easy for newcomers to "buy" land cheaply or to obtain ownership through complicated legal chicanery which the average man of those times neither understood nor cared about.

With political and social consciousness heightened by the Hawaiian Renaissance, it was inevitable that the question of reparation for the Hawaiian people would be raised. Hawaiians had seen the land rights of American Indians and Native Alaskans recognized and compensation made for past injustices. Through the efforts of many Hawaiian organizations, a Hawaiian reparation bill is now under consideration in Congress.

Kaho'olawe. Kaho'olawe is a small, uninhabited island off Maui's southwest coast. From the air it looks like the kind of Polynesian island people dream about. In reality, it is dry, dusty, and dangerous to walk on because of enormous quantities of unexploded bombs and shells accumulated over decades of military bombardment. Since World War II, the island has been used for target practice by U.S. Navy carrier airplanes and warships.

The bands of hardy goats, who have been the cause of much destruction due to their habit of cropping the already scanty vegetation too closely, were removed by the navy in 1980. It is hoped that with the removal of the goats, the land will once again support a fairly dense cover of plant life adapted to its dry climate.

According to archaeological investigation, the island had major religious and cultural importance and once supported a small permanent population. The island is also rich in unusual sites and artifacts that can illuminate periods of Hawaiian history that are presently a mystery. Years of bombing have endangered many of the ancient sites and made the island very hazardous. This destructive use of the land symbolized to many a total contradiction of the concept of "Aloha 'Āina." As a result, the island became a rallying point that called attention to the continued abuse of Hawai'i's limited land area.

In the 1970s, Hawaiian activists occupied the island to protest the bombing. Many members of the Protect Kaho'olawe Ohana were arrested; two, George Helm and Kimo Mitchell, disappeared while attempting to cross the channel on a surfboard. In 1990, President George Bush, Sr. ordered a moratorium on the bombing of Kaho'olawe. In 1993, Congress approved the return of Kaho'olawe to the State of Hawai'i, along with a program to clean up unexploded bombs and reforest the barren, forty-five-square-mile island. On May 7, 1994, the federal government formally turned Kaho'olawe over to the State. The navy removed its equipment and personnel, and relinquished access control to the island in 2004, though much unexploded ordnance remains buried there. The island is now being managed by the Kaho'olawe Island Reserve Commission, which continues its restoration.

"Aloha 'Āina" was one of the most crucial social and political issues of the nineties and it remains so today. Because of the debate over Kaho'olawe, the State has had to address the important question of proper usage of land in Hawai'i nei. Should social and spiritual aspects be considered as strongly as commercial potential for land? The way this question is answered will be of overwhelming importance for the future of Hawai'i. [Alexis Higdon]

Hawaiian Sovereignty

By the late 1980s, the Hawaiian Renaissance had evolved into the Hawaiian sovereignty movement. The quest for sovereignty, which once seemed relegated to the extreme fringe, became mainstream. Its defining moment came in January 1993, during the "'Onipa'a" commemoration marking the centennial of the overthrow of the independent Kingdom of Hawai'i. ('Onipa'a was Queen Lili'uokalani's motto and means "steadfastness.") The largest political demonstrations in state history took place at 'Iolani Palace, where ten thousand Hawaiians and their supporters rallied to protest the 1893 U.S.-backed coup. The massive demonstrations included an open air, theatrical re-enactment of the overthrow.

Then Governor John Waihe'e, a Hawaiian, ordered the removal of American flags from the capitol district during the hundred-year anniversary observances.

The 'Onipa'a mobilization marked a paradigm shift in Hawai'i's consciousness. Hawaiian sovereignty came of age, becoming a political force to be reckoned with. Then President Bill Clinton signed a joint Congressional resolution apologizing to the Hawaiian people for the illegal overthrow and the U.S.'s role in it. Hawaiian activists held a tribunal that found America guilty of war crimes and genocide against the kānaka maoli (Hawaiian people). From then on, there was no turning back. Beyond a general notion of sovereignty

as indigenous empowerment, the concept means different things to different parts of the Hawaiian community.

In 1996, ballots were sent out to about eighty thousand Native Hawaiians. Though respondents solidly supported Hawaiian sovereignty, few voted in 1998 to elect delegates to a Native Hawaiian Convention that would discuss the issue.

The Native Hawaiian Reorganization Act of 2007, more popularly known as the Akaka Bill, lays the foundation for a federally recognized government-to-government relationship between the U.S. and a Native Hawaiian governing entity. The bill has stalled in Congress.

The Akaka Bill is supported by the Office of Hawaiian Affairs. O.H.A. is also working to compile a registry of Hawaiians interested in self-governance as part of its Kau Inoa initiative. O.H.A.'s overall plan, called Ho'oulu Lāhui Aloha (to raise a beloved nation), calls for the designation of voter districts, and a constitutional convention to establish a Native Hawaiian governing body.

The most radical departure, advocated by activist attorney Hayden Burgess and Dennis "Bumpy" Kanahele of the Nation of Hawai'i, has been total independence, which would remove Hawai'i from the Union and reestablish Hawai'i as an independent nation-state, like the various members of the United Nations. Some within this faction favor democracy; others seek restoration of the monarchy.

During Onipa'a over ten thousand kānaka maoli and their supporters gathered at 'Iolani Palace to lament the overthrow of a nation and celebrate the possibility of restoration of sovereignty and self-determination. The streets of downtown Honolulu were blockaded by thousands of marchers and onlookers who joined Kia 'Aina (Governor) Mililani Trask and the officers and members of Ka Lāhui Hawai'i as they approached 'Iolani Palace. [Bruce Asato / Honolulu Advertiser]

A controversial and outspoken leader of the Native Hawaiian community, Haunani-Kay Trask is pictured here delivering an impassioned call for solidarity to achieve self-determination for Hawai'i's indigenous people. [Ed Greevy]

On August 29, 1992, the Halawa Coalition, a group of mostly Hawaiian women, blocked access to concrete delivery trucks heading toward a major concrete pour during the H-3 Freeway construction. The Coalition was resisting destruction of a newly discovered women's heiau, Hale O Papa. The freeway was rerouted because of concerns raised by the Coalition and others. [Ed Greevy]

Over four days in January of 1993, thousands of Native Hawaiians along with their supporters of all ages and backgrounds gathered at 'Iolani Palace to relive the overthrow of the monarchy and voice concern over injustices committed against the Hawaiian Nation. This historic "'Onipa'a" commemoration included a group of Roosevelt High School students who entered the Palace grounds with a greeting chant in honor of Queen Lili'uokalani. [Onipa'a Committee]

Islands in Transition

During the sixties and the early seventies, Hawai'i experienced unprecedented economic growth. Statehood and the inauguration of faster and larger airplanes led to tourism's quickly becoming Hawai'i's major industry, overtaking the sugar and pineapple industries, which had declined dramatically in the face of world competition.

There had been an earlier burst of economic activity during World War II, when the enormous military build-up increased population, employment, and construction. Hawai'i's population skyrocketed from 423,000 persons in 1940 to 859,000 in 1944. But by 1950, when the military presence had normalized, it plummeted to 500,000. In 1960, the state's population climbed to 633,000 and in 1970, to 770,000.

The rapid economic growth was accompanied by an unprecedented boom in construction. Because of inadequate planning and zoning regulations, growth often came at the expense of the environment. Projects were sometimes sited on what had been open spaces, mountain slopes, rain forests, and marshes. Country areas became suburbs, and suburbs became part of the city. New housing, higher incomes, more cars, increased government services, the revitalization of downtown Honolulu, and the massive build-up of Waikīkī reflected the state's unparalleled economic prosperity. Almost overnight, Hawai'i, which had known some hard economic times—particularly during the late forties—became one of the more well-to-do states in the Union.

Many groups bemoaned the growth process as important agricultural and beach lands were converted into suburban housing tracts and resort complexes, and low-income housing was demolished. On O'ahu, land eviction protests were staged, and whole communities rallied against land speculation and development. The political protests also fueled a renewed appreciation for Hawai'i's multicultural heritage. Music, literature, art, dance, song and comedy, the pride of being local, and the use of pidgin English became vibrant and creative ways to voice opposition to the injustices of economic growth.

During the 1980s, Japan's growing economy had a huge impact on Hawai'i. The strength of the yen dramatically increased property acquisitions by Japanese real estate firms who purchased "superblocks" in sections of Honolulu. The declining value of the dollar in Asia led to large-scale Japanese tourism, which changed the complexion of Hawai'i's visitor industry.

The eighties were also a time to honor Hawai'i's cultural roots. In 1985, the Japanese-American community celebrated its hundredth anniversary in the Islands with major public events, publications, and ceremonies. In 1986, the Chinese community commemorated its two hundredth anniversary in Hawai'i, and 1987 was designated the "Year of the Hawaiian." The eighties also saw Tom Selleck's *Magnum P.I.* replacing *Hawaii Five-O* as the most popular Island-based television program.

The optimism of the 1980s, which envisioned up to ten million visitor arrivals a year, dissipated in the 1990s with the Persian Gulf War and then Hurricane 'Iniki. Both depressed travel to the Islands, lowered hotel occupancy rates, and raised doubts about economic dependency on a single industry. When the "Japanese bubble" burst with the devaluation of the yen and the decline of the Tokyo stock market, investments from Asia suddenly dried up. Honolulu's "superblock" projects became empty lots overgrown by weeds.

The 1990s saw Pele erupting near Pu'u Ō'ō, covering the fields and homes of Kalapana with molten lava. Immigration from the mainland and Asia rose dramatically, and new faces and lifestyles changed Hawai'i's social climate.

The island of O'ahu, where over seventy percent of the state's population lived, became highly urbanized, a process that continues today. By the late 1990s, urbanization and resort development had spread to the former sugar fields of West O'ahu, where a "second city" at Kapolei emerged on O'ahu's 'Ewa Plains. Population growth and resort development also increased dramatically on the neighbor islands, particularly on the Big Island's Kohala Coast and on the south and west sides of Maui.

Hawai'i's population has been growing steadily: as of 2006, its resident population totals 1,285,000, with 1,241,000 local residents and 44,000 military residents. Additionally, on any given day, there are over 185,000 visitors present in the state.

As the first decade of the twenty-first century draws to a close, there is high economic growth fueled by a strong national economy. Real estate prices have increased dramatically during the last five years. In Honolulu, Waikīkī has been revitalized with new visitor facilities on Beachwalk Road. Upscale condos now fill the Kaka'ako and Kapi'olani districts. Throughout the state, luxury homes have sprouted at an unprecedented rate, drawing an influx of the rich from around the world. A mass transit system is planned to alleviate Honolulu's growing traffic congestion. Again, rural is becoming less rural, country less country—not just in Honolulu, but on the neighbor islands as well.

On the social and political fronts, the Hawaiian sovereignty movement shows increasing strength, and interest in Hawaiian culture is at an all-time high. In 2007, the admissions policy of Kamehameha Schools (which favors pupils of Hawaiian ancestry) was unsuccessfully challenged. The Akaka Bill, which attempts to redress injustices stemming from the illegal overthrow of the Kingdom of Hawai'i in 1893, has stalled in Congress.

The Waikīkī high-rise skyline is distinguished by the Rainbow Tower of the Hilton Hawaiian Village adjoining its lagoon on the left, and the Sheraton Waikīkī, in the center. The area's older landmarks, the Royal Hawaiian and Moana Hotels, are barely visible amid the concrete density. One architect of Waikīkī's phenomenal development was Roy Kelley, the "Wizard of Waikīkī," who helped launch nearly a dozen hotels between 1963 and 1974, including the Outrigger, Outrigger East and West, Coral Reef, Waikiki Tower, Reef Tower, Reef Lanai, and Waikiki Surf. [Warre R. Roll / Honolulu Star-Bulletin]

The Democratic Party, which governed Hawai'i until the election of Governor Lingle, is reorganizing. Voters are becoming increasingly unhappy with the costs of economic growth. And as the Asian military threat—perceived or real—persists, military expenditures (Hawai'i's second-largest industry) will remain important.

Hawai'i's multiculturalism continues to thrive. The Islands have one of the most distinctive blends of ethnicities in the U.S. and perhaps even the world. Almost half of the state's population is of Asian ancestry, and Hawai'i is the only state where Caucasians are outnumbered by non-Caucasians. Intermarriage shapes the cosmopolitan character of Hawai'i, with about fifty percent of marriages being interracial.

As Hawai'i moves toward the second decade of the twenty-first century, it will need to adapt to social, political, and economic changes while preserving its cherished way of life. If the past teaches anything, it is that Hawai'i will meet the challenges ahead.

Hawai'i's Governors

Hawai'i's current and last five governors testify to it's reputation as a true melting pot of races and groups. When Governor Burns died in office in 1973, then Lt. Governor George Ariyoshi took over the reins of the Democratic Party and the governorship. Often described as "quiet but effective," he won the 1974 election, becoming Hawai'i's first elected chief executive of Japanese-American ancestry. He won re-election again in 1982. At one point the Democratic Party machine was so strong it seemed that a Republican Party was unnecessary. His administration responded to growing criticism about too much economic development with a platform of "selective growth" and "diversification." [Hawai'i State Archives]

John Waihe'e with First Lady Lynne Waihe'e strolling across the grounds of 'Iolani Palace, at his December 1, 1986 inauguration. He was the first Hawaiian to be elected governor. [Ken Sakamoto / Honolulu Star-Bulletin]

In 1992, Benjamin Cayetano became Hawai'i's first governor of Filipino ancestry. He immediately faced a declining economy and the depletion of state revenues. During his 1998 re-election campaign, the Democratic Party, which had been in power for decades, came under fire from within and without. A rejuvenated Republican Party mounted a strong challenge and Cayetano won by only a narrow margin of votes. [George Kodama / Governor's Office]

Although Republican Linda Lingle (right), mayor of the County of Maui, narrowly lost her 1998 bid for governor, Island politics were entering an era of new political alliances. In 2002 she became the first Republican governor in forty years and the first female Hawai'i governor ever. She was easily re-elected in 2006. [Honolulu Star-Bulletin]

Governor Neil Abercrombie had served in Hawai'i's House of Representatives and Senate before serving in the U.S. Congress where he was re-elected ten times. In 2010, he won Hawai'i's gubernatorial election but lost the Democratic primary in 2014 to David Ige. [Ted Morita / Governor's Office]

Governor David Ige and First Lady Dawn Amano-Ige recite the Pledge of Allegiance during his inauguration ceremony on December 1, 2014. He is the first governor since Ben Cayetano to be born in Hawai'i and Hawai'i's second governor of Japanese descent. [Dave Au / Governor's Office]

ca. 300–700 AD	Polynesians from the South Pacific, most likely the Marquesas Islands, migrate in double-hulled canoes to the Hawaiian Islands.
700–1400	A distinct Hawaiian culture emerges as social classes are created and the ahupua'a, or land division, system evolves. Ali'i, or chiefs, rule pie-shaped units of land running from the mountains to the sea, worked by the maka'āinana, or the commoner class. Religious kapu, or laws, govern all aspects of life.
1400–1600	In an age of interisland wars, island kings consolidate their power as a complex system of religion and government emerges, and arts and customs flourish.
ca. 1736–1758	Kamehameha the Great, is born in Kohala on the island of Hawai'i.
ca. 1768	Ka'ahumanu is born on Maui. She will become Kamehameha's favorite wife and later, as kuhina nui, help the missionaries promote Christianity among her people.
1775–1779	Kalaniopu'u, ruler of the island of Hawai'i, and Kahekili, the ruler of Maui, engage in warfare.
1778	Captain James Cook encounters the Hawaiian Islands. He anchored off Waimea, Kaua'i (January 18) in the British ships *Resolution* and *Discovery* while en route from the South Seas in search of the Northwest Arctic Passage. • On his return voyage from the Northwest coast, Cook visits the island of Maui (November 26), and the island of Hawai'i (December 1). • The Hawaiian population is estimated by Captain Cook to be about four hundred thousand. (Recent scholars suggest that the correct figure may have been as high as one million.)
1779	Captain Cook anchors again in Kealakekua Bay, Hawai'i (January 17), where he is slain in a melee at Ka'awaloa, Kealakekua Bay (February 14).
1782	Kalaniopu'u, king of the island of Hawai'i, dies, leaving the districts of Ka'ū, Puna, and Hilo to his sons Kīwala'o and Keoua, and the districts of Kona, Kohala and Hāmākua to his nephew, Kamehameha. In the Battle of Moku'ōhai, Kamehameha defeats his cousin Kīwala'o and at the dedication of Pu'ukoholā Heiau at Kawaihae, Hawai'i, he slays Keōua.
1792	British Captain George Vancouver brings cattle and sheep to the Islands. Kamehameha I becomes sole ruler of the island of Hawai'i.
1794	Maui's Kahekili, ruler of Maui, Moloka'i, Lāna'i, Kaho'olawe, O'ahu, Kaua'i, and Ni'ihau, dies; Kamehameha conquers Maui, Moloka'i, Lāna'i, and Kaho'olawe. Captain William Brown of the British ship *Butterworth* visits Honolulu in December, becoming the first foreigner to drop anchor in its deep-draft harbor.
1795	Kamehameha conquers O'ahu.
1810	Kaua'i's King Kaumuali'i cedes his island to Kamehameha. • All of the Hawaiian islands officially become one kingdom under Kamehameha I.
1819	Kamehameha dies at Kailua-Kona, and his son, Liholiho, assumes the throne as Kamehameha II (May 8). Ka'ahumanu becomes kuhina nui. • The first American whaling ships visit Hawai'i. • Ka'ahumanu successfully urges Liholiho to publicly eat with women, an act previously forbidden under penalty of death. All kapu are overthrown and the king issues a proclamation to destroy all temples, thus stripping the nation of its official state religion.
1820	The first American Protestant missionaries arrive from Boston at Kailua, Hawai'i, in the brig *Thaddeus*. (March 31).
1821	The first house of Christian worship opens in Honolulu, on the site now occupied by Kawaiaha'o Church.
1823	King Kamehameha II (Liholiho) and Queen Kamāmalu sail for England where they succumb to measles.
1825	The first coffee and sugar plantations are started in Mānoa Valley, Honolulu. • Kauikeaouli ascends the throne as Kamehameha III. • Queen Ka'ahumanu converts to Christianity and enacts new laws throughout the Islands based on the Ten Commandments.
1827	The first Catholic missionaries arrive.
1830	Mexican and Californian cowboys arrive on the island of Hawai'i to help round up cattle. • Sandalwood forests become scarce.
1831	The Native Hawaiian population declines to 130,000.
1835	Large-scale sugar production begins at Kōloa, Kaua'i, using Hawaiian workers. • Hansen's disease (leprosy) appears in Hawai'i for the first time.
1839	Kamehameha III proclaims the Declaration of Rights, known as the Hawaiian Magna Carta.
1843	Lord George Paulet of England seizes the Hawaiian Islands and raises the English flag. • Admiral Richard Thomas of the British Navy repudiates Paulet's action and restores sovereignty to the Islands after Queen Victoria's personal intervention on behalf of the Hawaiian government.
1845	Foreigners are allowed to become naturalized citizens of Hawai'i.
1848	King Kamehameha III enacts the "Māhele," or division of lands, creating fee-simple land ownership among the king and chiefs. (January 27). • Epidemics kill thousands.
1850	Foreigners are allowed to own land.
1852	The first Chinese contract laborers arrive.
1853	Smallpox, or ma'i pu'upu'u li'ili'i, sweeps over the Islands, destroying many lives.
1863	Kamehameha IV dies at age twenty-nine. Prince Lot Kamehameha ascends the throne as Kamehameha V.
1866	Sufferers from Hansen's disease are sent to Moloka'i.
1868	The first Japanese laborers arrive.
1871	The Native Hawaiian population declines to seventy thousand.
1873	Prince William Lunalilo is elected king. • Father Damien, a Belgian priest, arrives at Moloka'i's Kalaupapa to minister to the sick.
1874	King Lunalilo dies without a designated heir, leaving the throne vacant again. • During a special session, the legislature elects as king, Prince David Kalākaua.
1876	A reciprocity treaty between Hawai'i and the U.S. allows Hawaiian-grown sugar to enter the American market duty-free.

1879	The first artesian well is drilled on Oʻahu. Such wells will allow thousands of acres of arid land to be converted into sugar cane fields.
1882	ʻIolani Palace is completed.
1885	The first company (944) of Japanese contract laborers arrives on the *City of Tokio* (February 9).
1890	King Kalākaua departs on the USS *Charleston* for San Francisco to receive medical treatment. • The Hawaiian population declines to forty thousand, making Hawaiians a minority group (forty percent).
1891	King Kalākaua dies in San Francisco at age fifty-four. • Liliʻuokalani becomes queen (January 29). • Princess Kaʻiulani, niece of the queen, becomes the heir apparent (March 9).
1893	Queen Liliʻuokalani's attempt to abrogate the 1887 constitution and proclaim a new one is thwarted as thirteen Honolulu businessmen organize the Committee of Safety (January 14) to challenge the queen's rule. • The committee takes possession of Aliʻiolani Hale, the government building, and proclaims that the monarchical system of government is abrogated, and a provisional government established in its stead until terms of union with the United States to be reached (January 17). The queen responds by yielding her authority to the United States Government until such time as the lawful rule of law is restored.
1894	The provisional government's President Dole declares Hawaiʻi a republic (July 4).
1898	Over twenty-one thousand Hawaiians and their supporters submit a petition to the United States government in opposition to annexation. Another seventeen thousand names on a petition request restoration of the monarchy. Unable to obtain a required two-thirds majority in the United States Senate for the Hawaiʻi Annexation Treaty, supporters of annexation pass a joint resolution of annexation which President McKinley signs at the White House (July 7). The validity of this joint resolution is used in lieu of an annexation treaty to annex the Hawaiian Islands.
1898 cont.	will be called into question one hundred years later by Native Hawaiians.
1899	Princess Kaʻiulani dies at the age of twenty-four (March 6). • The first case of bubonic plague appears in Honolulu (December 12).
1900	Hawaiʻi officially becomes a United States territory with S. B. Dole as first governor (June 14). • The first Puerto Rican workers arrive.
1901	The Moana Hotel opens (March 11), symbolizing the beginning of tourism as an industry.
1907	The first large group of Filipino immigrants arrives to work on sugar plantations.
1908	Work begins on Pearl Harbor naval base and dry dock. • The U.S. Pacific Fleet arrives from San Francisco.
1910	People of Japanese ancestry form Hawaiʻi's largest ethnic group in Hawaiʻi, accounting for 80,000 people, or forty percent of a population of almost 192,000.
1912	Duke P. Kahanamoku, Hawaiʻi's champion swimmer, goes to the Stockholm Olympic Games where he wins the hundred-meter race, establishing a world-record time. The people of Hawaiʻi accord him an "aloha" welcome at Honolulu and present him with a house and lot in Waikīkī.
1921	Reclamation of the Waikīkī swampland begins.
1925	The U.S. war fleet conducts notable maneuvers in Hawaiian waters (April).
1927	The Royal Hawaiian Hotel opens in Waikīkī (February 1).
1931	The infamous Thalia Massie kidnap-rape case attracts national attention.
1941	In the Japanese attack on Pearl Harbor, Schofield Barracks, Wheeler Field, Hickam Field, Kāneʻohe Naval Air Station, and Bellows Field, America suffers its worst military defeat in its military history as 347 airplanes are damaged or destroyed, six ships sunk, and 3,581 people killed or wounded (December 7). • Martial law is declared and a military governor assumes power.
1944	Martial law ends and civilian rights are fully restored.
1946	Three tsunamis hit the windward shores of the Hawaiian Islands, killing 159 people and causing $10.5 million in damage. • The 442nd Combat Regimental Team (which includes the 100th Infantry Battalion), "the most-decorated military unit in America's history," returns.
1959	The U.S. Congress passes a bill approving Hawaiʻi's admission into the Union of States (March 12). • President Dwight Eisenhower signs an admission proclamation and William Quinn (Republican) becomes Hawaiʻi's first state governor (August 21).
1960	Devastating tsunami waves strike the Islands, killing fifty-seven people at Hilo (May 24).
1962	Democrat John A. Burns defeats Republican Governor Quinn.
1967	One million tourists visit the Islands.
1971	Hilo's Merrie Monarch Festival hosts its first hula competition.
1974	George R. Ariyoshi becomes Hawaiʻi's first governor of Asian ancestry.
1976	The voyaging canoe *Hōkūeʻa* sails round-trip to Tahiti, confirming ancient Polynesian transpacific travel. • Hawaiian activists begin efforts to release the island of Kahoʻolawe from naval use.
1982	Hurricane ʻIwa strikes Oʻahu and Kauaʻi with winds as high as 117 miles an hour, causing an estimated $234 million in damage (mainly on Kauaʻi). As of 1982, it is the most destructive storm to hit Hawaiʻi (November 23).
1983	The official population of Hawaiʻi reaches 1,083,000. Ethnic distribution is Caucasian, 24.5 percent; Japanese 23.2 percent; Filipino, 11.3 percent; Hawaiian and part-Hawaiian, 20.0 percent. • Kīlauea Volcano starts the first phase of an island-building eruption that continues through the 1990s.
1985	The visitor count tops five million.
1986	John Waiheʻe becomes the first person of Hawaiian ancestry to be elected governor (November).
1992	Hurricane ʻIniki slams the Hawaiian Islands (September), devastating Kauaʻi.
1993	ʻOnipaʻa (stand fast) ceremonies held on the hundredth anniversary of the 1893 overthrow of the monarchy draw thousands of Hawaiians who mourn the events of the past while calling for a restoration of native sovereignty (January 17). • President Bill Clinton signs a congressional resolution acknowledging the illegal overthrow of the Kingdom of Hawaiʻi in 1893 (November 24).
1994	Ben Cayetano is elected Hawaiʻi's first governor of Filipino ancestry.

1994	Under a congressional appropriations act and presidential order, the island of Kahoʻolawe is returned to the State of Hawaiʻi.
1995	Pope John Paul II beatifies Father Damien in Brussels, Belgium.
2000	U.S. Senator Daniel Akaka introduces the Native Hawaiian Reorganization Act, known as the Akaka Bill, to provide federal recognition to native Hawaiians and protect federal funding of Hawaiian entitlements that were jeopardized by the recent U.S. Supreme Court decision in *Rice v. Cayetano*. The House of Representatives passes the Akaka Bill on October 24, 2007.
2002	Linda Lingle, the former mayor of Maui County, is elected governor of the State of Hawaiʻi, becoming the state's first woman governor and the first Republican governor in forty years.
2003	Federal spending in the State of Hawaiʻi totals $11.27 billion, including $4.84 billion in defense spending. Compared to other states, Hawaiʻi ranks sixth in federal spending, and second among all states in per-capita defense spending ($3,566).
2004	The annual visitor count for the Hawaiian Islands is 6,908,173, an 8.3% increase over 2003, shy of the record 6.95 million who visited in 2000.
2005	A panel of the 9th U.S. Circuit of Appeals rules two to one that Kamehameha Schools' 117-year-old policy of restricting admission to native Hawaiians is "unlawful race discrimination."
2006	Torrential rain pounds Oʻahu, wreaking havoc on homes, businesses, and streets. • The Akaka Bill falls four votes short of breaking a filibuster, preventing it from going to the Senate for a vote. Senator Akaka reintroduces the bill in 2007. • President Bush designates the Northwestern Hawaiian Islands Marine National Monument by signing Presidential Proclamation 8031. • A pair of early-morning earthquakes off the Big Island rattles much of Hawaiʻi. • A historic City Council vote approves a mass transit system the largest transit system ever approved in the state with an estimated price tag of nearly $5 billion. Many residents wonder if the city can afford to pay for the proposed 28-mile route and if enough people will use it.
2008	Genoa Keawe, longtime island entertainer, teacher, and mentor, dies at the age of eighty-nine. • In Rome, Pope Benedict XVI and Jose Cardinal Saraiva Martins promulgate a decree verifying two miracles attributed to Father Damien.
2009	One-third of the nation's endangered birds are in Hawaiʻi, threatened by destruction of habitat, feral animals and insect-borne diseases. • Pope Benedict XVI canonizes five new saints including Father Damien who had worked with Hansen's Disease (leprosy) patients on Molokaʻi.
2010	W. S. (William Stanley) Merwin, a Hawaiʻi resident of Maui since 1976, is named the seventeenth United States Poet Laureate. Hawaiʻi becomes the only state ever to have concurrently a U.S. President, a saint, and a poet laureate. • A "re-imagined" *Hawaii Five-O* television series premiers in the U.S. on CBS, 42 years to the day after the premier of the original show. (September 20) • Neil Abercrombie is elected governor.
2011	North Pacific Humpback whales now number over 20,000, about half of which visit Hawaiian waters. • Governor Neil Abercrombie signs Act 195 creating the Native Hawaiian Roll Commission that recognizes Native Hawaiians as the only indigenous people of Hawaiʻi who exercise sovereignty as a people, thus granting them status as a political entity and not just as a racial preference.
2011	A 9.0 magnitude earthquake off Japan's coastline causes a tragic natural disaster with massive damage and loss of life in Japan. Damages to Hawaiʻi ports, roads and homes resulting from the tsunami surges to the tens of millions of dollars. (March 11)
2012	Hawaiʻi's 7.89 million visitors tops the previous 2006 record of 7.6 million in 2006. Spending also reaches new highs with $13.9 billion in direct visitor expenditures. The recovering strong tourist industry helps the slumping state economy rebound. • A project to build Waikīkī's first oceanfront high rise hotel in more than three decades is cleared to move forward by the Honolulu Zoning Board of Appeals. (August) • Mainland billionaire Larry Ellison purchases the island of Lānaʻi from Castle & Cooke, Inc. owner David Murdoch for an undisclosed price estimated at more than $500 million. (June) • Waikīkī heeds a tsunami warning reminding Hawaiʻi again of its vulnerability to acts of nature. (October 27) • A 206-unit, luxury 17-story tower called One Ala Moana quickly sells out at record high prices. (November) • Oʻahu's $5.6 billion, 20-mile-long elevated-rail mass-transit project is allowed to proceed after prevailing in a federal lawsuit to halt the project. (December 27)
2013	The Hawaiʻi Community Development Authority, the state agency guiding development of Honolulu's Kakaʻako area, announces a draft of rules that allows the construction of high rise towers. (May)

Select Bibliography

Chinen, Jon. *The Great Mahele*. University of Hawaii Press, Honolulu, 1958.

Craighill Handy, E. S., and others. *Ancient Hawaiian Civilization*. C. E. Tuttle Co., Rutland, Vt., 1965.

Craighill Handy, E. S. and Pukui, Mary Kawena. *The Polynesian Family System in Kaʻu, Hawaii*. C. E. Tuttle Co., Rutland, Vt., 1972.

Daws, Gavan. *Honolulu—The First Century*. Mutual Publishing, Honolulu, 2006.

Daws, Gavan. *Shoal of Time—A History of the Hawaiian Islands*. University of Hawaii Press, Honolulu, 1974.

Day, A. Grove. *History Makers of Hawaii—A Biographical Dictionary*. Mutual Publishing, Honolulu, 1984.

Dorrance, William H. *Sugar Islands—The 165-Year Story of Sugar in Hawaiʻi*. Mutual Publishing, Honolulu, 2000.

Feher, Joseph; Joesting, Edward; Bushnell, O. A. *Hawaii: A Pictorial History*. Bishop Museum Press, Honolulu, 1969.

Grant, Glen; Hymer, Bennett. *Hawaiʻi Looking Back—An Illustrated History of the Islands*. Mutual Publishing, Honolulu, 2000.

Grosvenor, Gilbert M., Editor. *National Geographic Magazine*, December 1974.

National Geographic Society. Washington, D. C., 1974.

Kahanamoku, Duke with Joe Brennan. *Duke Kahanamoku's World of Surfing*. Grosset & Dunlap, New York, 1968.

Kuykendall, Ralph S. *The Hawaiian Kingdom*, 3 Vols, University of Hawaii Press, Honolulu, 1966–1968.

Nordyke, Eleanor C. *The Peopling of Hawaii*. University of Hawaii Press, Honolulu, 1977.

Scott, Edward B. *The Saga of the Sandwich Islands*. Sierra-Tahoe Publishing Co., Crystal Bay, Lake Tahoe, Nevada, 1968.

Simpson, MacKinnon. *A Century of Aloha—The Creation of Modern Honolulu*. Mutual Publishing, Honolulu, 2006.

Ten Bruggencate, Jan K. *Hawaiʻi's Pineapple Century—A History of the Crowned Fruit in the Hawaiian Islands*. Mutual Publishing, Honolulu, 2004.

The Ethnic Research and Resource Center. *The Portuguese in Hawaii—A Resource Guide*. Hawaii Foundation for History and the Humanities, Honolulu, 1973.

Trask, Haunani-Kay and Ed Greevy. *Kūʻē—Thirty Years of Land Struggles in Hawaiʻi*. Mutual Publishing, Honolulu, 2004.

Vandercook, John W. *King Cane—The Story of Sugar in Hawaii*. Harper & Brothers, New York, 1939.

Index

Joseph Mullins arrived in Hawai'i in 1967 but was a Polynesia-buff for two decades previously. As a marine in the southwest Pacific during World War II, he developed an abiding interest in the languages, culture, and archaeology of Polynesia and Melanesia. He spoke Tongan and Spanish the last a result of his studies at the Universidad Nacional Autónoma de México. His previous books included *Treasury of Ancient Hawaiiana, King Pine,* and *Hawaii Planner.* As well he contributed articles to *Honolulu Magazine* and served as public relations advisor to the Fiji Association of Hawai'i, in cooperation with the government of Fiji. He recently passed away in Chicago, the city of his birth.

Mutual's illustrated historical narratives include *Hawai'i Looking Back: An Illustrated History of the Islands; Maui Remembers; Pearl Harbor—From Fishponds to Warships; The Hawaiian Monarchy; Kohala 'Āina: A History of North Kohala; A Century of Aloha: The Creation of Modern Honolulu;* and *Big Island Journey.* For more information including how to order, visit www.mutualpublishing.com or contact Mutual by email at info@mutualpublishing.com or Mutual Publishing, 1215 Center Street, Suite 210, Honolulu, Hawaii 96816.